YUGOSLAVIA

BULGARIA

MACEDONIA

THRACE

Thessalonike   Kavalla

CORFU I.

MT.
OLYMPUS

THASOS I.

Gulf of Salonika

MT.
ATHOS

IONIAN
IS.

THESSALY

AEGEAN

LEMNOS I.

N. SPORADES
IS.

CEPHALONIA I.

MT.
PARNASSUS

EUBOEA I.

Gulf of Corinth

Patras

Delphi

Eretria

LESBOS I.

SEA

ZANTE I.

CHIOS
I.

Corinth

Mycenae
Nauplia
Sparta

Thebes
Marathon

PELOPONNESUS

Athens

ANDROS I.

N

Messene

MYKONOS
I.

CYCLADES IS.

S. SPORADES IS.

0   50   100

Scale of Miles

SANTORIN I.

DODECANES IS.

CRETE

Heraklion

RHODES I.

Knossos

MEDITERRANEAN SEA

ALBANIA

EPIRUS

GREECE

TURKEY

THE HORIZON CONCISE HISTORY OF

GREECE

by Alexander Eliot

Published by
AMERICAN HERITAGE PUBLISHING CO., INC.
New York 1972

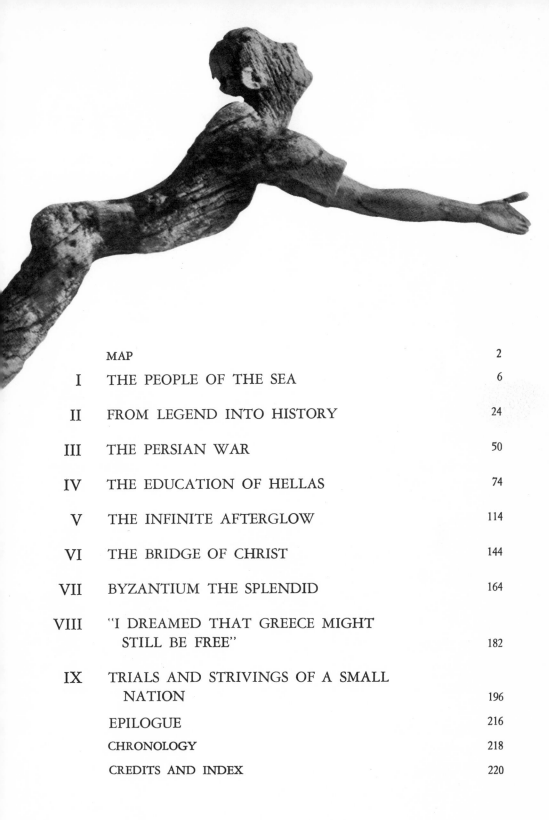

CHAPTER I

THE PEOPLE
OF THE SEA

Greece is the southeast corner of Europe and the cornerstone of Western civilization. Tremendous cultures of ancient times played into what is now Greece. They were the Mesopotamian civilization of the Two Rivers, and that of Egypt. Herodotus, "the father of history," rather shocked his contemporaries by maintaining that all of Greece's best ideas came from Babylon and Memphis. But of course Herodotus himself proved otherwise. He invented history of a detached, detailed, delightful and nonbraggart sort. He drew much of his information from the Near East and from Africa, but what he did with it was new, was Greek; it was the beginning of a discipline which lives on. Herodotus' storytelling quality, and his simple felicity of style, still constitute an ideal for historians. It is worth noting, too, that Herodotus was born in Ionian Greece, on what is now the western coast of Turkey. He traveled very widely and finally came to rest at Athens, where he probably wrote his great *History of the Persian Wars*. In similar fashion, Greek culture as a whole drew from the entire then-known world and reached its fullest bloom at Athens. Geography made this the natural development. From a Near Eastern perspective, the Greece of prehis-

*A fifth-century-*B.C. *bronze, representing either the god Zeus or Poseidon*

toric times was not a land mass but an island-studded sea. This sea, the Aegean, cradled a very lighthearted, glorious, and peaceful trading culture long before Athens came to be.

This "Third Culture," as the historian James Henry Breasted called it, will be the main subject of the present chapter. "Besides the two older centers of civilization on the Nile and the Two Rivers [Tigris and Euphrates]," Breasted says, "there grew here in the Eastern Mediterranean the splendid world of Crete and the Aegean. It is this third great civilization which forms the chief link between the civilization of the ancient Near East and the later progress of man in Greece and Western Europe." But before taking a close look at the relics of that lovely, long-since-vanished link, let us embark on a brief tour of the islands that nourished it and of the Greek mainland beyond.

The Aegean resembles a lake in some ways. It forms a rough rectangle bounded on the north by the coasts of Macedonia and Thrace and on the south by the island of Crete. The Anatolian coast is its eastern border and the coast of the Greek mainland stands opposite. In between lie hundreds of islands, large and small. When sailing the Aegean one is almost always within sight of land. One cruises from island to island in a matter of a few hours. The largest of the islands, Crete and Rhodes in the south, are rich in vineyards and olive groves. The smaller archipelagoes, such as the Cyclades in the central southern Aegean, are chiefly rich in physical beauty. Largely bare of trees, sculptured by salt winds and wine-dark seas, they sometimes resemble fragments of heroic sculpture. Their whitewashed villages also are sculptural, and it is said that the modern architect Le Corbusier received his chief inspiration on a visit to the island of Mykonos. The sea is poor in produce and always has been so. Its deep blue color which reminded Homer of the dusky grape, betrays an absence of the microscopic green marine life required to support a large fish population. The islanders therefore must supplement what night fishing they do with income from sheep and goat herding, sponge fishing, sailors' remittances, and especially tourism. They are the guardians of as yet largely unspoiled Edens for vacationers. But it is a question whether these island Edens are going to stand for long against the incursions of steadily accelerating industry and tourism. However, on many islands one may still discover villagers living about as their forefathers did thousands of years ago.

The Peloponnesus, which literally means "Pelops' isle," constitutes the southernmost quarter of mainland Greece. It takes the name from the legendary Eastern hero who first brought civilization there. The Gulf of Corinth makes a blue slip between it and the Balkan Peninsula proper. Since the digging of the canal across the Isthmus of Corinth at the gulf's eastern end (an engineering feat which the Roman Emperor Nero tried and failed to accomplish and which British dynamite finally brought off), "Pelops' isle" has been made in fact an island. Its central province is a mountainous region still partly forested with oak and beech and inhabited by a poor, brave, hard, warm sort of people who remind one of Appalachian mountain folk. Like the Hatfields and McCoys, their clans also engage in blood feuds, and male children are welcomed into the world as "new guns."

Arcadia is the ancient name of the central Peloponnesus. South of that region lies "the Hollow Land," as the ancient Spartans called their home. It is a beautiful valley, rich in orange groves, cupped by the awesome Taygetus peaks. To the west of Arcadia, near the coast, is Olympia. The register of victors in the original Olympian Games, which were held at this place, gave classical Greece its chronology. As we date things from the birth of Christ, classical Greece dated them from the first Olympian Games, which were held in the year 776 B.C. Some traces at the site take the imagination back almost that far, but the most impressive remains are from the early fifth century B.C. Among them is the temple of Zeus whose columns stand some thirty-four feet high. There were a hundred and thirty-four columns orginally. This temple was cast down in the fifth century A.D. at the behest of the passionately antipagan Byzantine emperor Theodosius II, and its steps served merely as a resting place for shepherds for more than a thousand years. In the nineteenth century, German archaeologists excavated the site and partly restored the temple of Zeus. They even managed to piece back together the sculptures from the temple's pediments. In those of the west pediment, which depict the struggle between Lapiths and Centaurs over the Lapith women, marble is made to writhe like limbs of olive trees. The Cambridge critic Charles Seltman places this unexpectedly expressionistic work at the peak of all Greek carving.

Turning now to the opposite, eastern coast of the Peloponnesus, one descends from the Arcadian highlands to the Argolis, a word which appears to mean "Plain opening on the sea." At Nauplia, the port of the Argolis, modern Greece had its original capital. Its first president, Capodistrias, was assassinated there in 1831. The constitutional monarchy which has been so controversial a part of modern Greek politics began with King Otto's disembarkation at Nauplia in the year 1833. The harbor boasts a pretty little castle which dates from the days of Venetian rule. The battlements above the town on the steep headland were constructed by Venetian and Ottoman conquerors. Inland from Nauplia lies a market town near the site of ancient Argos, whose cone-shaped acropolis dominates the plain. Beyond that again, the Cyclopean fortress of Tiryns sleeps like some giant land tortoise. According to legend, Tiryns was once home to the demigod Heracles—better known in the West by his Latin name, Hercules. The palace may date from the fifteenth century B.C., or even earlier. It is no wonder that later Greeks thought giants must have built the palace; its walls measure more than fifty feet thick at some places and are constructed of granite blocks up to ten feet long. Behind Tiryns, in a high corner which commands both the plain and the pass to the north, is fabled Mycenae. Here the sons of Pelops held sway between the years 1600 and about 1200 B.C. According to Homer, Mycenae alone contributed no less than a hundred ships to the siege of Troy.

The pass to the north, which Mycenae guarded, opens out onto the rich gulf coast of the Peloponnesus and the isthmus which hinges Pelops' isle onto the soil of Attica. Corinth controls the hinge, or did in ancient times. The town is of small importance today. But her immense acropolis used to be called the northern horn of Pelops' isle. (The southern horn was 2,630-foot Mount Ithome in Messenia.) "Not everybody gets to Corinth," Cicero said. But during the days of Roman domination Corinth was Greece's greatest tourist attraction. This seems to have been thanks primarily to the compliant priestesses of Aphrodite who inhabited the Love Goddess' luxurious and immense temple overlooking Corinth. Getting there involved a long, steep climb but travelers from all over the known world pronounced it worth the effort.

Crossing the Corinthian Canal, one enters Attica by way of a winding coastal highway. This used to be a dangerous stretch until the Athenian hero Theseus destroyed Procrustes and the other ogreish villians who infested it. Passing the Strait of Salamis one cannot but think

Cloud-capped Mount Olympus in Thessaly, dwelling place of the gods

back to the day when a comparatively puny Greek navy, under the guiding genius of Themistocles the Athenian, almost entirely destroyed the proud Persian armada of the emperor Xerxes in the narrow passage. Tradition relates that Xerxes himself witnessed the holocaust from a throne set up on a high point of this coast. Tears of rage and shame doubtless stung his eyes. As the Athenian tragedian Aeschylus put the case in his surprisingly sympathetic play *The Persians:* "There never yet 'twixt sunrise and sunset perished so vast a multitude of men." One reason was that the Persians, unlike the defending Greek sailors, did not know how to swim. The coast road continues down into a rather smelly and heavily smogged region of cracking plants, shipyards, and soap factories. A few marble remains, a shallow cavern, and a small wooded hill form a tiny oasis in this industrial purgatory. They are what is left of Eleusis, the site of the mysteries of the Corn Goddess Demeter and her daughter Persephone. For more than two thousand years this was a spiritual center for the entire pagan world.

Passing on up the ancient Sacred Way from Eleusis toward Athens, one is tempted to pause at the little Byzantine church and monastery of Daphne. This architectural gem contains some of the most exquisite sacred fresco and mosaic art surviving from Byzantine times. In the shadow of its walls, once a year, Athens conducts a rather elaborate and jovial wine festival. This festival puts one in mind, nostalgically, of Attica as it appeared a scant decade ago. The countryside about Athens lay open then. Athens was violet-crowned, as the poet Pindar long ago described it. The purple hills which ringed her plain were murmurous with the sound of bees and heady with the scents of rosemary, basil, and thyme. The air was so clear that one could actually count from some distance away the leaves on a particular olive tree. But now no more. Athens has swelled almost beyond recognition to include almost a quarter of the present Greek population. It is a proud, messy, modern metropolis complete with traffic jams, which radiates for miles and miles in every direction from the ancient Parthenon.

Herman Melville, the far-traveled author of *Moby Dick,* once stood upon Athens' Acropolis looking northward to the scarred slope of Mount Pendeli (ancient Pentelikon) from which the Parthenon's marble came. The mountain seemed to him, he wrote in his notebook, like a mother gazing down upon her child. Pendeli is like a mother not only

Hephaestus, god of smiths, is shown hammering in the bronze at left. Hermes, god of shepherds and flocks, carries a ram in the statue at right.

to the Parthenon but also to Athens and the Attic plain as a whole. This will still be true centuries from now. Pendeli looks southward upon Athens and eastward upon the beach of Marathon. On that beach in 490 B.C. the sons of Athens, although outnumbered ten to one, drove an invading Persian force into the sea. The northern slope of Pendeli faces the Boeotian plain where Hesiod the ancient poet practiced husbandry. He pronounced the region hot in summer, cold in winter, and barely tolerable at any season. But as one takes the road once more, northward through Thebes, it seems like Paradise Regained. This is prosperous although windswept and thinly populated country. The big sky overhead and the strong various colors of the hills remind one now and then of Wyoming. On the left Mount Parnassus, 8,060 feet high, may well be wearing a round snowcap on its clear blue brow. Hidden in a cleft of Parnassus, on its southwestern side, is Delphi, once the Vatican of the whole pagan world. Pushing on to the north one comes to the rock pinnacles of Meteora, each capped by a medieval monastery. These sandstone formations were apparently shaped by the waves of a prehistoric sea. Rising hundreds of feet high in such a way as to over-hang the plain dramatically, they seem almost like monolithic arms and hands making silent gestures of prayer. The monasteries used to be reachable only by drawbridges, rope ladders, and pulleys operated from above. Today one can ascend most of the way by road and go the rest by steps cut in the rock. Just a few Orthodox monks and nuns remain to tend the gardens and sound the bells half way between earth and sky, but they are wonderfully hospitable to the pilgrim.

Northward again one crosses the plains of Thessaly where in 48 B.C. Pompey and Caesar fought for control of the Roman Empire. Rugged Mount Olympus rises more than nine thousand feet against the northern sky. The Olympian pantheon of Greek deities received its name from Mount Olympus, whose summit was supposed to underpin the gods' abode. The gods have long since departed but Mount Olympus naturally remains sacred in its own changeless way. Olympus now shows a new face as a place of Christian pilgrimage: in common with hundreds of mountains in the Greek Orthodox world, it has its chapel dedicated to Elias, the Greek Elijah.

North of Olympus, at the head of the Gulf of Salonika, lies the second city of modern Greece, Thessalonike. Beautifully situated, bustling, industrial, Thessalonike indeed resembles a miniature Chicago. Its population stands at about half a million as against two million and more for Athens. No other Greek city compares with these in size; nor is any other so plainly a part of the modern age.

But now let us wipe the Greek slate clean of man's work. Thessalonike does not exist, nor does ancient Athens or ancient Mycenae. This whole country is uninhabited, or nearly so. We stand twelve thousand years ago in time. Northwest of Thessaly, in the narrow valleys of Epirus, Stone Age food gatherers huddle and romp and chip flints before their limestone cave dwellings. These are barely glimpsed through the millennial mists, and are gone again. Then, soon after the year 7000 B.C., Stone Age farmers begin pushing into Europe and Asia across the Bosporus. By 6500 they have established an extensive settlement northwest of what is to become the city of Thessalonike. Their cabins are of brick built on foundations of stone. They possess sheep and goats, and it appears that they sow barley, peas, beans, and emmer (Eurasian wheat) in rotation. They build shrines, almost certainly, as homes for baked clay statuettes of what seems a burstingly fat fertility goddess. For century after century their settlements in northern Greece survive. These rise like the Hill of Hissarlik (which archaeologists found to conceal the seven superimposed cities called Troy). But Stone Age Macedonian communities are fearless; no fortifications constrict them. The people are without weapons. They have no knowledge of the wheel, not even the potter's wheel. Yet their baked clay pots are beautiful and the seasons lap them in peace. Theirs is the Golden Age and it goes on, for three thousand years and more. Later Greek legend will look back longingly to that more ancient time.

Far to the south, on the island that is now called Crete, comparable settlements appeared as early as 5000 B.C. The people had come there by ship, apparently from the Levant, bringing with them pigs, sheep, and cattle. It seems that the mastery of the sea which was to be the distinguishing characteristic of these people had very early beginnings indeed. They too, like their mainland cousins half a world away to the north in Macedonia, lived without fortifications and created fat fertility goddess figurines. Among their earliest settlements on Crete were two which would eventually shine in glory: Knossos on the north central side of the island and Phaistos on the south. A scant 180 miles' sea journey lay between Crete's southern coast and Africa, where Egyptian civilization was soon to flower. To the northeast lay Rhodes and the Anatolian coast, no more than a hundred miles distant. To the northwest the Cyclades and mainland Greece were within still easier reach.

The Cyclades came to predominate over Crete itself with the dawn of the Bronze Age. At Melos, for example, men were mining obsidian and trading in copper and gems long before their neighbors to the south or on the Greek mainland. From about 3000 B.C. the Cyclades islanders extended their prospecting and mining operations and their trade in obsidian blades, metals, and craft objects in every direction. New archaeological evidence makes it fairly certain that these people, who must never have been numerous, adventured at last as far west as Spain. Copper was rare enough; but tin, which must be combined with it to make bronze, was still rarer and more difficult to find. Egypt and Sumer alike lacked these metals and both had need of them. So the miners and mariners of the Cyclades came to fill a vital middleman function between the civilizations of Asia and Africa and the still-barbarous north and west. The art of these people was modest, small in scale, and simple, yet at the same time it achieved a purity and rigor all its own. Modern taste, conditioned by such twentieth-century masters of abstract sculpture as Brancusi and Picasso, stands utterly astonished by the refinement of certain marble carvings from the Cyclades.

The culture of the Cyclades mingled with that of mainland Greece to create what is now known as the Helladic civilization, characterized by citadel building and the interment of the noble dead in vaulted stone tombs. Thus the heroic age came to Greece. Cattle raiding, armed combat, sieges, war and warrior cults appeared. The fertility goddess of former times slowly gave way to semidivine sons and grandsons with bronze-tipped spears.

Meanwhile, to the south of the Cyclades in the large fertile, sea-cradled island paradise which Crete seems to have been, a culture of a sunnier kind sprang into being. Sir Arthur Evans, whose excavation of Knossos in 1900 first revealed the existence of this maritime civilization, called it Minoan. The name refers to the legendary Cretan king Minos who was said to have conquered ancient Athens and sacrificed the flower of Greek youth to his bullheaded son—the Minotaur—which he kept imprisoned in an architectural maze known as the laby-

Cult images of the mother goddess took such varied forms as the bare-breasted faïence figure from Crete at left, and the Cycladic stone idol at right.

rinth. Prince Theseus of Athens, according to myth, defeated the purposes of King Minos by seducing his daughter the Princess Ariadne. The princess had the wit to provide Theseus with a ball of thread when he entered the labyrinth. By attaching one end of the thread to the gate of the maze and unrolling the rest as he wound his way inward to the Minotaur's lair, Theseus was able to escape the place once he had destroyed the monster. The hero brought Ariadne away with him from Crete but soon afterward abandoned her. Among the many curious episodes embedded in this legend is one which describes a dance performed by Theseus on the island of Delos in the northern Cyclades. The dance, composed of many hesitations and turns, was understood to represent precisely Theseus' trials in the labyrinth.

Evans himself reckoned that the huge and luxurious palace of Knossos which he excavated was itself the labyrinth. It had many levels, courtyard after courtyard, winding corridors, and a profusion of light-wells to serve as windows on the sky. Its bathroom arrangements were as elaborate as one might find in a grand hotel of the twentieth century. Its cellars contained rank upon rank of man-high jars filled to the brim with olive oil, grain, and wine. Its red-painted columns tapered toward

Three terra-cotta figures from a Minoan votive group dance around a lyre player.

the pedestals in which they were socketed—rather like the "morning-glory columns" which Frank Lloyd Wright invented for his Johnson's Wax Building. The rooms, like the vaults of Egyptian tombs, were lavishly decorated with scenes from nature, everyday life, and festivals. Wasp-waisted cupbearers and bare-breasted courtesans swarm through the few paintings which Evans found remaining under the earth.

The most astonishing and famous of the lot seems to depict athletes leaping across the horns of a bull. Sport of this kind appears impossible to modern rodeo performers and bullfighters. Not even El Cordobes or Dominguin would dare try somersaults up and over a charging bull. Yet it is at least conceivable that the Cretan bulls did not charge in anger; they may have been trained to perform their part in the festival. In fact it may have been not so much a murderous struggle between man and beast as a deliberate expression of amity in power—an admittedly dangerous but harmonious dancing of young men and women with the mighty bulls. The awe-inspiring palace of Knossos had no battlements at all. It pointed no admonishing tower nor aspiring steeple to the sky. Instead, the structure wore at its crest an arc of sculptured horns, which Evans called the Horns of Consecration.

All these factors doubtless did play into the myth of Theseus and the Minotaur. Yet they hardly begin to explain the story. There seems a harsh and gloomy cast, somehow, upon the imagination which created the legend. And, on the other hand, gloom is notably absent from the culture which has been revealed at Knossos and her sister city Phaistos. Minoan civilization possessed a quality of its own which can be summed up in a single word: dance. Compare, for example, the four-square grandeur of the pyramids or the Assyrian ziggurats to what was constructed at Knossos. Contrast the staring stillness of Mesopotamian idols and votive figures, or the rigid clenched-fist poses of the pharaohs at Memphis and Luxor, with the fluid, breeze-teased and seemingly debonair graces of Minoan art. Something new comes into being here and it is just the opposite of monumental. Motion, made to look easy but performed according to highly precise principles, is the key to Minoan art. I dare to suggest that it may prove a useful clue to the whole culture and history of prehistoric Crete.

By the twentieth century B.C., Crete was the kingpin of a giant thalassocracy. (The word comes from the Greek *thalassa,* for "sea," and denotes a sea empire.) Minoans traded in Rhodes, Cyprus, Sicily, Ischia and the Bay of Naples, Marseilles in what is now France, and the coast of Spain, with permanent trading posts becoming colonies in some instances. Small kingdoms or baronies allied to the Minoan cause existed on the Cyclades islands and at Tiryns, Mycenae, Pylos, Thebes, and Orchomenus on mainland Greece.

In Crete itself there now appeared what the archaeologist Gordon Childe has called an urban revolution. Knossos became the center of a city and port with possibly a hundred thousand inhabitants. A paved road connected it with the island's summer capital, Phaistos in the south. Dozens of new towns arose, each dominated by a luxurious palace or manor house. Aqueducts were built. Where small bronze daggers had been worn, swords now appeared for the first time; but still there were no fortifications anywhere on the island. Craft objects and works of art were produced in quantity for overseas trade. Cretan craftsmen worked with ivory and blue faience paste imported from Egypt as well as with gold and gemstones from the north. At this time, too, written notation in a pictograpic style somewhat reminiscent of Egyptian hieroglyphs came into use on Crete. This earliest writing, which archaeologists have labeled Linear A, has yet to be deciphered. It may be seen impressed on a round clay tablet from Phaistos, now in the Archaeological Museum at Heraklion. The ideograms on this disc were imprinted by separate molds. Each one is thought to represent a syllable and they are set forth in a spiral. Since the signs are rhythmically arranged with repetitions of what appear to be refrains, the text may well constitute some invocation or hymn. No one knows whether the spiral ought to be read from the edge to the center or the opposite.

The failure of all attempts so far to crack Linear A leaves yet another intriguing mystery about Minoan civilization. Egypt and Mesopotamia, the parents of this strange sea-born third world, left massive monuments and rock-cut inscriptions galore, as if determined to cast long shadows into history. Just the opposite is true of the Minoan thalassocracy. This new civilization stood for movement as against monumentality. Its open cities and palaces were built for beauty and convenience rather than to impress; characteristically, Minoan architecture was helter-skelter. Again, the wealth of this new civilization lay not in fertile and almost changeless land but in small portable things

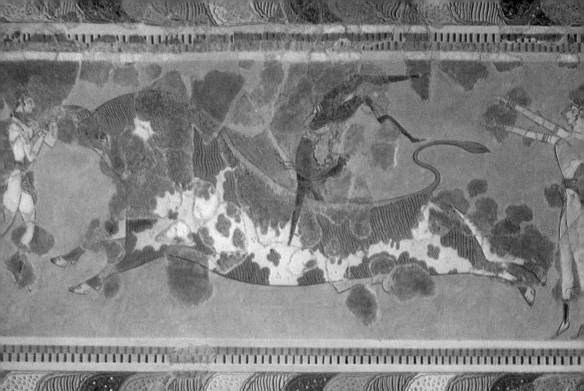

carried to and fro in trade across the trackless sea. Minoan heroes cannot have been conquerors, since weapons appear only very late in the development of this civilization; they were explorers and entrepreneurs. If bull, dove, partridge, monkey, dolphin, and the like throng Minoan art, the commonest animal of all to be found there is the modest and mysterious octopus. Consider what a contrast that makes as a symbol to set against the winged bulls of Babylon or the Egyptian sphinx. "The hairless one, the boneless one, who gnaws his foot in a sunless house," thus Hesiod described the octopus. But the Minoans obviously saw this fellow being in quite another way: as the sinuous and secret lord of the hidden reefs.

In a cataclysmic moment which still reverberates through the minds and myths of men although it has never yet been satisfactorily pinned down, the reef which had been home to the silver-tentacled Minoan octopus shook itself apart. Earthquake, fire, and flood destroyed it. Angelos George Galanopoulos, director of the Athens Seismological Institute, estimates by radio carbon dating that the event happened no earlier than 1500 and no later than 1300 B.C. Professor Spiridon Mar-

A fresco from the palace of Knossos in Crete depicts intrepid Minoans at their ritual sport—somersaulting over the backs of sacred bulls.

inatos, the distinguished archaeologist who is now engaged in excavating the site of the disaster, says his finds favor the 1500 date. On the other hand John Godolphin Bennett, chairman of the British Center for Comparative Studies in History and Philosophy, prefers a mid-fifteenth-century dating since this would fit best with the story of the parting of the Red Sea in Hebrew chronology and also the story of Deucalion's Flood in Greek chronology. Professor Galanopoulos has himself proposed with great conviction that legendary Atlantis actually existed in the eastern Mediterranean and was in fact Minoan, and that it did sink beneath the waves much as legend describes.

The Greeks are no strangers to earthquakes. Among the ancient Greek writers, Pausanias perhaps succeeded best in conveying their awesomeness. "Warnings, usually the same in all cases," he wrote, "are wont to be sent by the god before violent and far-reaching earthquakes. Either continuous storms of rain or else continuous droughts occur before earthquakes for an unusual length of time, and the weather is unseasonable. In winter it turns too hot, and in summer along with a tendency to haze the orb of the sun presents an unusual color, inclining to red or else to black. Springs of water generally dry up; blasts of wind sometimes swoop upon the land and overturn the trees; occasionally great flames dart across the sky; the shapes of stars too appear such as have never been witnessed before, producing consternation in those that witness them; furthermore there is a violent rumbling of winds beneath the earth." All these signs and more must have astonished and terrified the eastern Mediterranean world in the months preceding the explosion which was to come. As Dr. Bennett has pointed out, the Seven Plagues of Egypt may well have been among the actual portents. But now let us for a moment step out from under the cloud of dread which enveloped the world at that time. We are on Santorin (the ancient Thera), a crescent-shaped island whose jagged ridges are actually the crown of a profound underwater volcanic crater, in the southern Cyclades. Under a brilliantly blue sky, Professor Marinatos and his team are delicately delving into the rosy pumice. Already these excavations have yielded Minoan ceramics, furniture, and bronzes of a high order, plus wall paintings in earth colors and crushed lapis lazuli which are so fine, free, filled with motion and sweet feeling as to surpass anything of their kind, including even the first of the paintings uncovered at Pompeii. They constitute the best evidence yet found for the notion that Thera was Atlantis and the doomed hub of the Minoan world.

The crater under what is now the harbor of Santorin exploded with a force estimated at three times that of the Krakatoa eruption of 1883. After the Krakatoa explosion two-thirds of that twenty-one-square-mile island collapsed inward leaving a crater a hundred and sixty fathoms deep. Some 36,000 people were drowned by the resulting tidal waves along the neighboring coasts of Java and Sumatra. The explosion was heard two thousand miles away in Australia. At distances of a hundred miles and more the shock waves alone smashed window-panes and cracked walls. Floating pumice up to thirteen feet thick covered the sea for miles around Krakatoa. The volcanic ash hurled aloft eighteen miles and more turned day into night over a two hundred and seventy-five mile radius. For months afterward the whole world knew sunrises and sunsets of an unprecedented feverish redness.

Krakatoa has become a part of modern scientific legend, and rightly so. But just imagine what an eruption three times as great taking place at the height of the Bronze Age and in the very cradle of civilization must have been like. The Santorin crater is five times greater in volume than that of Krakatoa. The thickness of the ash thrown out of Krakatoa nowhere exceeds sixteen inches, whereas at Santorin it lies as much as a hundred and thirty feet thick. Undoubtedly it devastated the entire north coast of Crete with fire and flood. It must have wreaked incredible havoc all around the Aegean and literally joggled three continents: Asia, Africa, and Europe. Almost all the ships in the Mediterranean that were lying inshore or in harbor at the time must have gone down. Most docking facilities and seaside markets were surely destroyed. As for what may have been the actual capital of the Minoan thalassocracy at Thera, it simply disappeared; partly under the sea and partly under a vast, thick shroud of pumice. Small wonder that the Minoan empire never recovered from this cataclysm. Not even the Minoan way of life survived. The rough fragments of the thalassocracy wrenched apart. Fragment by fragment, they would now build a new world; a world no longer bent upon commerce, art, and enjoyment. The ethos of the coming age would result in one thing: war. But let that be the subject of our next chapter.

CHAPTER II

FROM LEGEND
INTO
HISTORY

The fourteenth century before Christ witnessed the takeover of Mycenae and other mainland Greek citadels as heirs to Minoan civilization. Mycenaean culture was oriented more to hunting, piracy, and war than it was to commercial and festive pursuits. This in itself made a return to the Golden Age of Minoan times out of the question. Yet Mycenaean art and religion, at least, preserved much. The Mycenaeans conquered Crete itself, and then adventured on eastward to the island of Cyprus (for its copper) and all the way westward to the Cornish coast of England (for its tin). Civil struggles at home, which culminated in the siege of Thebes by Peloponnesian forces and the siege of Troy by a twelve-hundred-ship expedition under the Mycenaean king Agamemnon, almost exhausted Mycenaean power during the next hundred years or so. Then came the Dorians, down from the north, with iron weapons, and with wagon trains carrying their women and children. They meant to stay, and stay they did. Every Mycenaean stronghold except Athens fell. The Dorians even crossed the sea southward to Melos in the Cyclades and from there to Crete which they in turn conquered. They never advanced eastward to Cyprus, however,

A helmeted warrior, carved in marble, from the temple pediment at Aegina

and they left much of the Anatolian seacoast to be colonized by Mycenaean refugees. They let trade go entirely. Phoenician merchantmen moved out from Tyre and Sidon in Lebanon upon the abandoned sea lanes. Centuries passed. Dozens of Greek towns formed pocket governments led by men rich enough to afford horses, body armor, and weapons; one might call them knights. By the eighth century B.C., the tunnel of Dark Age life opened onto new vistas of a startling sort. Younger brothers of the knights migrated abroad with sword in hand to seek their fortunes. Amazingly, they conquered and held coastal settlements right around the Black Sea, in southern Italy and Sicily, and along the Mediterranean coast of France, Spain, and Libya. At home, meanwhile, the religious mystery centers at Olympia, Delphi, and Eleusis developed and propagated new world views. Writing, which had vanished from Greece, returned. But the new Greek alphabet was Phoenician. Homer and Hesiod sang. Lyric poets such as Archilochus and Sappho followed. In Ionia, on the eastern side of the Aegean, philosophy and science came to be practiced. At Athens under a lawgiver named Solon, something like democracy was born.

There you have, all in a rush, the current of Greek triumphs and defeats between about 1400 and 500 B.C. In the course of nine centuries, the Greek-speaking peoples stumbled from heroic heights into total obscurity, and came back stronger than ever, ready to fling wide the gates of Europe and take a leading part in shaping the modern world. It is a rather inspiring story that this chapter has to tell, so let us look at certain aspects of the drama in more detail.

First, the Mycenaeans: historians call them that in preference to the more technical term "Late-Helladic People" because Mycenae itself has yielded the richest remains of their culture. But were the far-flung conquerors, traders, and pirates of the Mycenaean era actually ruled from one citadel overlooking the Argos plain? This is not possible to tell from the few records that remain. The evidence points rather to a feudal organization involving dozens of petty kingdoms and innumerable semi-independent baronies. Yet Egyptian and Hittite documents of the period indicate that Mycenaean power must have been sufficiently cohesive to win respect in Africa and Asia. Pharaoh Ramses III actually contended with Mycenaean invaders of the Nile Delta. His archers won the day. But not long afterward, it seems, Mycenaeans conquered the Egyptian province of southern Syria. The region was to be known by their tribal name, for these "Philistines"—Greek "Pelasgians"—long dominated Palestine.

Sometime about the year 1300 B.C., a Hittite monarch sent certain letters to the "King of Ahhiyawa." Philologists identify the Ahhiyawa people with Homer's Achaeans. The Hittite communications complain of piracies and usurpation in what seems to be the city of Miletus and along the Lycian coast. Intriguingly enough, they point to intimate relations between the royal families of Greece and Anatolia. The Hittite monarch's tone is friendly and respectful; he reminds the Achaean king of former days when they rode together in the same chariot. A later letter from King Tudhaliyas IV (1250–1220 B.C.) to one of his allies mentions "the kings who are of equal rank to me: the King of Egypt, the King of Babylon, the King of Assyria, and the King of the Ahhiyawa." The picture which emerges from all this is of a world where no sharp distinction between East and West yet exists. Mycenaean kings seem to have lived in somewhat the same style as those of the Hittites, not to mention the lords of the scattered coastal cities and islands in between their two countries.

Where writing was used only for official business, differences of language were probably less important than they seem to us. The same holds true for differences of religion. Some Greek myths can be shown to stem from Hittite sources, and others from Egyptian. More to the point, the Greeks for their part assumed that the gods of other nations were really their own under various odd aliases. The Greek legend which tells of the Olympian gods hiding out in Egypt for a while under the guise of animals is one example. This seemed to explain the animal-headed deities which Greek traders, tourists, and mercenaries came upon in Egyptian temples.

Mycenaean art itself owed far more to the vanished Minoan world than to Asia and Africa. A famous pair of golden cups from Vaphio (near Sparta) in the National Gallery at Athens represent wasp-waisted youths catching and taming wild bulls. It is Minoan in the lightness of the figures, and in the ritual quality of the action as well.

Equally impressive are certain Mycenaean gems engraved with images of a Mother Goddess—or "Lady of the Labyrinth" as one inscription declares her to be. These derive through Cretan prototypes from the most ancient idols known in Greece, the fat fertility figures of Neolithic times. Mycenaean art shows her bare-breasted as a rule, with animal companions. As ruler of subterranean regions and queen of all earthquakes, she would often appear with serpents twined around her gleaming lifted arms. As guardian of the earth's surface, mountain goddess, and monarch of the beasts, she would sometimes stand on the shoulders of lions, or she would step between a pair of lions rampant and gently hold them apart. As goddess of the sky, giver of love, and bearer of invisible seedlings, she would come with doves perched on her shoulders. Or sometimes she bestrode a goose, like the mysterious mother-figure in children's fairy tales. Her hair was usually ringleted and long, her skirt bell-like, her breasts brimming, and her eyes wide.

The Mother Goddess clearly must have been the chief deity of the Mycenaeans. But she was not the only one. The fairly recent decipherment of Mycenaean writing, Linear B, has turned up a number of names from the Olympian pantheon which Homer knew. Among them are Zeus, Hera, Poseidon, Hermes, Athena, and Artemis. The double-axe symbol which frequently appears in Mycenaean art is thought to relate to the thunderbolt of Zeus. But the Mycenaean Zeus may well have been a "Dying God" on the Asiatic model represented by Adonis, or the Egyptian Osiris; that is to say, a cyclical nature force who was worshiped as Child, King, and Sacrifice, each in turn, over and over.

The Mycenaeans spoke the same language and shared some of the same deities with the Dorian invaders who were to destroy them. Moreover they were warriors heart and soul, at least as much so as their conquerors-to-be. And finally they had the advantage of a high civilization and very mighty fortresses to defend them. This raises an intriguing question. Namely, why did the Mycenaeans suffer abject defeat at the hands of such poor relations? The answer given used to be that the Dorians possessed iron weapons whereas the Mycenaeans did not. The whole thing turned, according to this theory, on technology. But iron is the democratic metal, easy to find and to mine. Moreover, steel was not yet known. An untempered iron sword would bend and break as readily as a bronze one. The answer, then, must have been more political than technological. The Mycenaeans seem to have torn their own social fabric to shreds in the course of small civil wars. The ten-year siege and final sacking of Troy was one such struggle. Furthermore the

Mycenaeans may not have dared arm their peasantry against attack, for fear of insurrection. Mycenaean nobility, as Homer makes clear, fought according to certain rules—man against man—for booty and for fun. The Dorian invaders were more serious. They needed land, desperately, to grow food on which to live. Their families came with them, and every man advanced armed to the teeth. So the Mycenaeans were overwhelmed.

The Dorians practiced few crafts and less trade. They let the old Mycenaean palaces lie abandoned. These people may actually have preferred village life, farm work, and obscurity. Each Greek valley had its huddle of huts, and every huddle owed allegiance to a local *basileus,* or chieftain. Sometimes one village fought its neighbors, bitterly, but not for glory. No more than a tenth of the Greek countryside consists of alluvial valley, earth suitable for cattle raising and subsistence farming. The rest is mountains and thin-soiled limestone hills. Olives and

Death masks, like the golden "Mask of Agamemnon" shown here, were placed upon the faces of Mycenean monarchs during the burial ceremony.

grapes may thrive on the hillsides, but these are special crops. Sheep and goats do well on barren heights but they denude the soil still further, and returns on them are meagre. So good bottom land was what the Dorians battled over, from village to village. Hunger was their one common enemy. From the archaeological standpoint they produced nothing of note except pots. Decorated in the severe "geometric" style with circles, stripes, and checkerboard patterns, Dorian ceramics create an impression of uncompromising austerity. Their funerary vases achieved giant proportions. By the ninth century, they began to include stick figures of beasts and men, corpses and mourners, between the lines. These elaborately organized creations of baked and painted clay pointed forward, in a way, to the similarly large-scale triumphs of Homer's and Hesiod's poetry.

Homer was probably an Ionian Greek of the eighth century B.C. Tradition calls him a son of the island of Chios, which lies off Izmir (formerly Smyrna) on the west-central Anatolian coast. His ancestors may well have been among the many Mycenaeans who fled before the Dorians to begin life over again along the eastern edge of the Aegean Sea. Homer's first great epic, the *Iliad*, tells of a cruel climax in the Trojan War which took place some four centuries previous to the poet's own time. It draws upon legend and oral history alike, impartially. In spirit, the epic is still Mycenaean. "Sacker of cities" is an expression of praise, not blame, in Homer. But love and peace and the virtues which pertain to them are also to be found woven into the *Iliad's* blood-soaked tapestry.

Homer dared use the gods as comic relief. Deities decide much of the action in the *Iliad*, but they do so arbitrarily and for reasons ranging from the all-too-human to the contemptible. Homer's gods are extreme personalities who happen to possess powers analagous to those of Superman and Wonder Woman in our comic books. Did the poet or his readers believe in them? Probably so, but belief need not imply self-abasing reverence—let alone love. Greeks stood up to the gods which Greeks themselves had made. Their ancestors, they said— on Homer's good authority—had walked and talked and even fought spear to spear with the willful children of Zeus.

The *Odyssey*, Homer's second epic, concerns the long home-coming of his favorite hero from Troy. It tells how Odysseus was constrained, in part by the enmity of the sea-god Poseidon, to wander the western Mediterranean for ten long years. Fabulous folk tales of lotus-eaters, one-eyed ogres, and a man-transforming sorceress play into this poem. But a good deal of enigmatic mariner's lore is in it also. Perhaps Homer had access to a Phoenician pilot's guide. In his time, Greeks themselves were just beginning to dare the waters of the western Mediterranean once more after a lapse of centuries.

Contemporary with Homer, or not much later, there lived a poet whom the Greeks themselves considered to be very nearly Homer's equal. His name was Hesiod, and his works still survive. One hears little about them, partly because they prove so difficult to translate. But the main reason for the obscurity of Hesiod's name today is that he had less humanly interesting tales to tell than did Homer. Hesiod was a small farmer by trade. He lived in Boeotia, one of the most fertile regions of mainland Greece. (Boeotia may be translated to mean "Cow-country.") Hesiod's interests, aside from writing poetry, were first theology and second agriculture. He wrote long poems in epic style on each of those themes. As in the case of Homer, Hesiod's diction too was rapid, plain, and noble all at the same time. But where Homer tended to praise all things from weapons and horses on up, Hesiod took a darker view. His *Theogony,* a genealogy of the gods, is a thunderous tempest of sex and violence. His *Works and Days,* on the other hand, can be read as a kind of farmers' almanac stuffed with wry home truths. Gods and mortal men, Hesiod maintains, both sprang from Mother Earth. For a long time the world was a kind of garden in which men at least, though not the gods, lived at peace with one another. Such was the Golden Age. A Silver Age followed, characterized by a sort of childish impiety and quarrelsomeness. People no longer lived as long as their ancestors had done. A Bronze Age succeeded the Silver and brought with it what Hesiod calls "the lamentable works of war." The men of this time were hard of heart "like adamant," Hesiod says. They ate no bread; their armor, their tools, and even their houses, were all of bronze. They had no iron. They destroyed each other. Then came a race of heroes and demigods, and this—Hesiod tells us—was the generation before his own. "Some of them met grim war and its battle-fates: in the land of Kadmos at Thebes with seven gates they fought for Oedipus' flocks disastrously, or were drawn to cross the gulf of mighty sea for sake of Helen tossing her beautiful hair." But, Hesiod goes on, the gods transported some survivors at least to Islands of the Blessed in the midst of the ocean, where there is no sorrow and crops come up three times a year. As for his own generation of men, the poet simply despaired of it:

> *This is the Race of Iron. Dark is their plight.*
> *Toil and sorrow by day are theirs, and by night*
> *the anguish of death; and the gods afflict them and kill,*
> *though there's yet a trifle of good amid manifold ill.*

One has the feeling, reading his account, that Hesiod looked back with clear vision upon immense vistas of time. His picture lacks detail, but it jibes well with the findings of recent archaeology. As for Hesiod's view of the world around him, it was sharply focused. Later Greeks relished Hesiod's advice for its rare blend of shrewdness and dignity. He was not fooled and yet he never fell into mere cynicism.

The expansive and rather optimistically tumultuous mood of Greece in the seventh century B.C. can almost be summed up by the single figure of Archilochus—poet and soldier of fortune. Archilochus came from the island of Paros in the Cyclades. His father was an aristocrat; his mother probably a slave. His best friend was his spear. While soldiering in Thasos, he fell in love with a girl named Neoboule and immortalized her in just a handful of haunting lines. She turned him down all the same, whereupon Archilochus aimed such savage satires at her that she hanged herself.

Archilochus has been called the first lyric poet. Homer and Hesiod claimed to take dictation from the Muses, figuratively at least. The things they wrote about were common property. But Archilochus sang of private matters; his art was the cry of his own heart. Yet sentimental he was not. Nor was he at all self-indulgent. Archilochus concentrated; he made himself a burning glass of his own passions without losing the ability to laugh at himself. This is rather a fine point, perhaps, and yet crucial to the development of Greek literature, and our own as well. Professor Werner Jaeger of Harvard explains that Archilochus "learned how to express in his own personality the whole objective world and its laws—to represent them in himself. Personality, for the Greeks, gains its liberty and its consciousness of selfhood not by aban-

Proud lionesses surmount the gate leading into the ancient citadel of Mycenae.

doning itself to subjective thought and feeling, but by making itself an objective thing; and, as it realizes that it is a separate world opposed to the external law, it discovers its own inner laws."

Having lived by the spear, Archilochus died the same way. An adventurer like himself, nicknamed the Raven, struck the poet down. Afterward the Raven turned up at the shrine of Delphi to ask a question. Before he could open his mouth, however, the oracle cried out: "You have slain the Muses' servant, the man of utterance. Depart from the temple." This story shows with what reverence the ancient Greeks, even as far back as the seventh century B.C., regarded poetry. The Delphic oracle belonged to the god Apollo, who was himself a singer and poet. Delphi was to be the center of Greek thought and religious life for a long time to come, as we shall see.

If Archilochus has the distinction of being the first lyric poet, Sappho of Lesbos remains by common consent the best in Greek. "The Tenth Muse," Plato called her. She lived only a generation after Archilochus, but her island corner possessed a peacefulness such as her predecessor never found. Sappho ran a sort of finishing school for "Servants of the Muses"—meaning young ladies. She made them feel that they were also servants of the Graces, and of Aphrodite, the Love Goddess. Her school prepared one for marriage, so it was only natural that some of her poems should be addressed to favorite pupils on the eves of their weddings. She herself was married, and the mother of a little girl whom she compared to an armful of golden buds. A contemporary described Sappho as being short and dark, "like a nightingale with misshapen wings"; but others call her the "beautiful Sappho." Her love lyrics burn like the pale calyxes of small dark flowers found under a hedge.

Obviously, Sappho must have adored certain girls in her charge. Sexual love between women is called "lesbian" still, because Sappho was a native of Lesbos Island. But the very intensity of her love poems transcends sex per se. Just like "the dear good angel of the spring, the nightingale"—to quote one of Sappho's most haunting lines—she seems a sheer voice sweetly flowing from impenetrable shade. "Of all the poets of the world," as John Addington Symonds wrote, "Sappho is the one whose every word has a perfection and inimitable grace." It is no wonder that the ancient Greeks, who often referred to Homer simply as "The Poet," honored Sappho likewise as "The Poetess."

About the middle of the seventh century, the kings of Lydia in Asia Minor began to mint coins. The Greeks immediately seized upon and imitated this new invention. Money was to become as revolutionary a force as writing itself. By adapting the Phoenecian alphabet to their own purposes a century previous, the Greeks had already created an immortal literature. Now, while one Greek city-state after another issued its own currency, Greece bloomed anew as a commercial power. Miletus on the eastern side of the Aegean, and Athens on the west, quickly developed the banking and borrowing and insurance techniques required for high-risk enterprises overseas. Small manufacturers prospered. The peasantry diminished as the urban proletariat and the slave population grew. Clever upstarts became millionaires, while many a gallant knight of the old school, as the poet Theognis complained, was

Broken by poverty, made weak,
Denied all power to act or even speak.

In Sparta the new commercialism seemed to create more harm than good. Sparta's position was a peculiar one, of course. Her people were pure Dorian, proud of their toughness and their rough manners. They had acquired the fertile lands of the native Helots whom they more or less enslaved, and also of the neighboring Messenians, most of whom they reduced to the level of sharecroppers. But still Sparta was land-locked and made few exportable goods. By contrast to the burgeoning economy of Athens to the north, Sparta seemed poor. Spartan nobles who indulged in the new fashion for luxurious living ruined themselves and further weakened the whole community. The poor Helots who tilled the land for their Spartan masters were rebellious. So, too, were the conquered Messenians nearby. All in all, the situation at Sparta appeared ripe for disaster. However, a legendary knight named Lycurgus moved to stop fate, locally at least, and thus rescue Sparta. Tradition relates that Lycurgus had traveled to Crete, Ionia, Egypt, and even distant India in search of the best laws for his city. He went last to the oracle of Apollo at Delphi.

Lycurgus went home possessing a code of laws as astonishing as they were severe. When he entered the Spartan Senate to explain just

what he had in mind, a brawl ensued. One of his eyes was struck out by a stick, but Lycurgus eventually won the day. He declared, first, that Sparta would have to use iron ingots worth only a few pence to the pound. Secondly, Lycurgus demanded that the sons of Sparta be taken from their mothers at age seven and reared to one profession only: soldiering. The armed-camp manner of life which Lycurgus imposed was "Spartan" indeed. It did create the only standing army and by far the most formidable fighting force in Greece. Sparta's heavily armed "hoplites," or foot soldiers, did, moreover, succeed in keeping down the Helot serfs and Messenian subjects. There was oppression, but no beggary; everyone ate. Spartan government was cruelly severe and Spartan economy was closed up tight, but for all that the Hollow Land prospered after its own fashion. In years to come, Sparta would excite not only awe but also the warm admiration of most Greeks. The political philosophy represented there was to play into Plato's *Republic*. It would influence Roman, Moslem, Fascist, and Communist legislation.

The story of how Lycurgus met his end may not be altogether reliable. He is said to have requested a leave of absence from the soldier-society which he had brought into being. That granted, he exacted a solemn vow from his fellows that they would stay true to Sparta's new rule of life until such time as he reappeared in their midst. Then, legend says, Lycurgus stole quietly away and starved himself to death. For generations the vow which had been made to him was kept.

Athens, meanwhile, engaged in a territorial war with a neighboring

*A scene from a sixth-century-*B.C. *vase painting depicts Greeks and Trojans fighting for the body of Achilles who lies dead on the battlefield of Troy.*

city, Megara. The island of Salamis was the prize in dispute. Megara won the war, whereupon the Athenians passed a law forbidding any citizen to raise once more the old claim to Salamis—on pain of death. But a young merchant named Solon had the courage and ambition to defy that decree. One day in the *agora,* or market place, of Athens he pretended to go insane. Leaping up on a marble block which was reserved for the use of official heralds only, he recited a poem. It was a call to resume the war with Megara. Instead of putting him to death as required under the law, the Athenians cheered Solon for having dared say under the guise of madness what they themselves also desired. War was resumed, and Solon commissioned as a general. Taking only a small detachment of men, he marched to Cape Colias where the women of Athens were performing rites of sacrifice in honor of Demeter, the Corn Goddess. Solon had purposely chosen beardless youths for this expedition. Interrupting the rites, he had his soldiers array themselves in the women's flowing robes and headdresses. Each man kept a dagger concealed in his skirt. The soldiers then frolicked along the beach, in plain sight of the Megaran garrison on Salamis Island, which was just across the strait. The ruse was successful; the Megarans embarked in order to kidnap what they thought were defenseless Athenian women. Running their ship up onto the beach in the very midst of Solon's girlish troops, they were cut down to the last man.

In Solon's time, three factions contended for political dominance of Athens. The landed aristocracy were the conservative right wing of

Athenian politics, bitterly opposed by poor peasants and the burgeoning urban proletariat on the radical left. Between the two stood a small party of enlightened businessmen with Solon at their head. The situation was as explosive in its way as the one which Lycurgus had overcome in Sparta. But here the dangers arose from economic and legal causes rather than from military exploitation. A conservative leader named Draco had saddled Athens with a terribly severe legal code designed to protect wealth and property, and to discourage any citizen from taking independent action publicly. Whether for pinching a pomegranate from a market stall or for murdering a rival in love, the penalty was the same: death. "Draconian" remains in the legal lexicon to this day. It means law and order carried to the point of no return.

But Draco's code was not all that distressed the Athenian underdogs. As money grew to be the common medium of exchange, the rich and powerful became ever more firmly entrenched while the poor stumbled blindly into debt. Small peasant holdings on the Attic plain were mortgaged and foreclosed continually. Poor people sold their children into slavery, and they themselves were often enslaved for nonpayment of debts. Yet they vastly outnumbered the rich, of course, and under the Athenian constitution they too were citizens—at least so long as they retained their freedom. The radical left clamored for redress. They wanted nothing less than a clean slate in Attica, with the land parcelled out anew to give every citizen his fair share. And so the crisis mounted; revolution appeared imminent. That was the position when Solon, the wily general and self-made merchant prince, achieved the leadership of the Athenian Assembly.

Solon came to power as a compromise choice. The rich were ready to accept him because he too was rich, and the poor were willing because Solon was a man of principle. The story goes that Solon, like Lycurgus before him, consulted the Delphic oracle in order to learn what he should do. "You are the pilot of Athens," the oracle told him. "Take the tiller firmly. You have many friends in the city." This pronouncement may well have been what gave Solon the extraordinary courage required to disappoint everyone. Grasping the helm of his ship of state, Solon steered the vessel directly between the conservative reef and the radical whirlpool. He disappointed the poor by not redistributing land. At the same time, he infuriated the rich by simply canceling all debts

The legendary Trojan horse, concealing Greek soldiers inside, was mistakenly accepted by the Trojans as a peace offering.

which were owed them. Further, he ordained that no Athenian citizen should ever again be enslaved for nonpayment of debts. He invited home again all who had suffered exile for the same failure. He unearthed the stones engraved with mortgage notices throughout the Attic plain. He repealed capital punishment except in the case of homicide. He took a census of the Athenians and afterward allotted particular privileges to each man according to his wealth. Even the poorest were assured of a vote in the Athenian Assembly and were expected to perform jury duty. This meant the beginning of popular democracy as against mere factional strife.

Solon remarked that the best-governed city in the world would be one "where those who had not been wronged showed themselves just as ready to punish the offender as those who had been." To this end, he decreed that anyone who presumed to remain neutral in a crucial public dispute would thereby forfeit citizenship. Such were the most important regulations instituted by Solon, but it appears that his new code of laws was rich in curious details as well. Any man who marries an heiress, Solon insisted for example, should be required to have intercourse with her at least three times a month. Another of his laws which cannot really have been enforceable was much admired for its inherent logic. Namely, that no one be permitted to speak ill of the dead. Solon's reasons for this were first that piety requires us to regard the dead as sacred, second that justice calls upon us to refrain from attacking those who have no means of defending themselves, and third that political good sense suggests that we ought not be allowed to perpetuate ancient grudges.

Solon's code was duly inscribed on wooden tablets and set up in a public place. The Assembly approved it entirely, "for a hundred years." But so many citizens came to Solon's door with questions and complaints regarding one law or another that he soon determined to get out of town. Making his commercial interests an excuse, he obtained a ten-year leave of absence from Athens. He sailed first to Egypt, where he spent some time in study and discourse with the high priests of Heliopolis and Saïs. According to Plato, these Egyptian hosts instructed Solon in much ancient history which the Greeks themselves had long since forgotten—including the story of how Atlantis sank beneath the waves. From Egypt Solon proceeded to Cyprus, where he

Cadmus, the mythological founder of Thebes, is portrayed slaying a dragon.

supervised the planning and foundation of a new city. In gratitude, the king of Cyprus named the city after him.

According to legend, the rich young kingdom of Lydia, in Asia Minor, was Solon's next stop. He was magnificently entertained by Croesus the king, whose wealth remains a byword to this day. But Solon seemed not in the least dazzled by the Oriental luxury of the Lydian court, and this put Croesus in a pet. "Tell me," Croesus demanded, "have you ever seen a human being more fortunate than I am?" Solon said yes to this. He mentioned three people he knew, none of them rich or famous, who had died nobly with their good names intact. Croesus lost his temper. No doubt Solon's attitude seemed disrespectful to the king, and his explanation provincial. But Solon coolly stood up to the red-faced and glaring monarch and offered him some unasked-for observations. Solon's words on the occasion, as reported by Plutarch, have a truly Greek ring.

"King of the Lydians," Solon began, "the gods have given us Greeks only a moderate share of their blessings, and in the same way our wisdom is also a moderate affair, a cautious habit of mind, I suppose, which appeals to common people, not a regal or magnificent one. This instinct of ours tells us that human life is subject to innumerable shifts of fortune and forbids us to take pride in the good things of the present, or to admire a man's prosperity while there is still time for it to change. The future bears down upon each one of us with all the hazards of the unknown, and we can only count a man happy when the gods have granted him good fortune to the end. To congratulate a man on his happiness while he is still living and contending with all the perils of the mortal state is like proclaiming an athlete the victor and crowning him before the contest is decided; there is no certainty in the verdict and it may be reversed at any moment."

These remarks left Croesus cold. Solon took his leave. When he finally got back to Athens, he found that fortunes there were changing fast. A demagogue named Pisistratus was abusing the democratic machinery in order to concentrate real power in his own person. To clinch matters, Pisistratus staged a fake assassination attempt upon himself. Despite Solon's warnings, the Assembly voted to provide Pisistratus with a bodyguard of fifty men for his own protection. Before they knew it, Pisistratus had raised a private army and seized the Acropolis.

He became "Tyrant"—a Greek word meaning king in all but name.
Solon spoke publicly against him, but Pisistratus simply smiled and
consolidated his own position. Thereupon the old legislator went
home and took down the armor which he had worn as a young general.
He laid this in the street before his door. "I have done all that was in
my power to help my country and uphold its laws," he declared, and let
the matter go at that.

Pisistratus represented the wave of the future for sixth-century
Greece. Chiefly by capitalizing on the discontent of the poor, tyrants
were able to override the right-wing knights and seize control in city
after city. Some tyrants were evil men, while others earned legendary
reputations for wisdom and goodness. Pisistratus himself proved to be
far from the worst. He encouraged the arts and commerce so effectively
as to assure Athens' future greatness. Moreover, he retained most of
Solon's laws, and treated the retired sage with every respect.

It was about this time that Athenian drama began. An innovator
named Thespis, none of whose works have come down to us, produced
and performed in tragedies honoring the god Dionysus. Old Solon disapproved of this. He asked Thespis whether he were not ashamed to
tell such lies in front of so many people. The dramatist replied of
course that one should distinguish between lies and make-believe.
Solon angrily struck the ground with his staff and exclaimed in a
cracked and quavering voice: "That's all very well, but if we permit
ourselves to praise and honor make-believe the next thing will be to
find it creeping into our serious business."

Perhaps Solon was thinking of the make-believe by means of which
the tyrant Pisistratus had come to power. In any case, he had a point.
Greek imagination and Greek realism could and did make a highly
volatile combination. This mixture played, for example, into the mysteries performed at Eleusis fourteen miles from Athens' gate. The rites
which were held at Eleusis each year honored Demeter, the Goddess of
Corn and patroness of agriculture, and Persephone her daughter who
was lost and returned again like seed sown in the ground. Participants
in these rites began by learning certain secrets of nature and agriculture
which would make them more effective and whole-souled children of
the land. But as the years went by, the mysteries performed at Eleusis
developed into religious drama of a secret and obviously inspiring sort.

OVERLEAF: *Dionysus, god of wine and merrymaking, accepts a libation from a
comely maenad in this detail from a vase painting.*

DATE DUE

4 Aug 81			
GAYLORD			PRINTED IN U S A

Initiates were somehow brought to the point of believing that they themselves were Persephone's children and Demeter's grandchildren —that they were, in a word, immortal. The assurance of happy immortality of the soul which was propagated at Eleusis ran counter to the harder and humbler view of the human condition which Solon had expressed in his advice to Croesus. This contradiction is built into classical culture at its very foundations.

But now let us return to the eastern shores of the Aegean, which were dominated by Croesus the Lydian. For it was there that philosophy as such came into being. The first person named in Diogenes Laertius' *Lives of Eminent Philosophers* is Thales of Miletus—an engineer who served King Croesus. Thales had studied mathematics in Egypt and astronomy at Babylon. He flabbergasted his contemporaries by accurately predicting an eclipse of the sun in the spring of 585 B.C. But by way of laughing off that seeming miracle, people said that he once fell into a well while taking observations of the stars. The canard contained a modicum of poetic justice, since Thales insisted that water must be the primary material of the whole universe. This contention might seem at first glance to involve a long step back from the mathematical and astronomical sophistication which Thales had gained in Egypt and Mesopotamia. But in fact it represented a new departure for science, into physics. Hesiod had said that Oceanus was a very great progenitor. The Babylonians maintained that their god Marduk had first "made the dry land appear" out of the flood. Thales' great contribution to such poetry-of-evolution was simply that he eliminated gods from the picture. Water, he said, in effect, makes its own changes by means of inherent natural processes. Heated, it turns to mist, while sufficient cold solidifies it into ice. A host of subtler transformations, invisible to the eye but definitely not supernatural, are what create all things out of primal water, so Thales maintained. People called him a dreamer, naturally, but he refuted that by making a fortune in the olive oil trade. When Lydia fell before the advancing hosts of the Persian conqueror Cyrus, Thales proposed that the Ionian states of the seacoast form a federation to resist the invader. The idea had never been broached before, and it got nowhere. Cyrus attached the cities of Ionia, including prosperous Miletus, to his immense but loosely pulled-together empire. Thales died of sunstroke at a ripe old age, having come

to the conclusion, according to Laertius, that the easiest thing in the world is to give advice and that the hardest is to know oneself. This more than anything else, perhaps, truly earned him the title "philosopher," which in Greek means simply a "lover of wisdom."

Anaximander, a disciple of Thales, greatly refined the master's imaginative physics: not water but something indefinable, "the indeterminate," is the primal substance. All things, including man, are so to speak momentary condensations, or clouds in the heaven of the divine. Coming to be and passing away, Anaximander added, occur according to a universal law of compensation: what is born must die, or rather make way for birth. This led him to the concept that all creation is comprised in a "cosmos"—or "perfect order" as the Greek word signifies.

After Anaximander came a third Ionian philosopher with a confusingly similar name: Anaximenes. He disagreed about the original material of the world. Isn't "the indeterminate" in reality some sort of rarefied and invisible mist? In fact, why not say "air"? Air, to the Greeks, meant soul as well. It was literally "the breath of life." And therefore in the last analysis air seemed to Anaximenes not only matter but the divine afflatus at the same time. This brought matter and spirit, science and religion, to the same thing in a way. His doctrine, as Theodor Gomperz observed, "affords a foretaste of the atomic theory, a conception of the material world which, whether or not it pronounces the last word on the subject, has at least proved down to contemporary times an invaluable aid to philosophy. It detracts but little from his claim to immortality that Anaximenes took the trouble to support his teaching by miserably misunderstood experiments."

Pythagoras of Samos seems to have possessed the universal genius of a Leonardo da Vinci. Like Leonardo's world, the one in which Pythagoras grew up was dominated by glittering tyrants who showed devotion to the fine arts. Polycrates, the dictator who ruled the island of Samos and the neighboring Ionian coast around 535 B.C., had made his court the cynosure of Greece. He imported architects who designed some of the first classic Greek temples, and sculptors who brought the lost wax technique of hollow bronze casting from Egypt to Greece. Last but not least, Polycrates' engineers managed to run a nine-hundred-foot water tunnel through a hill into his capital. The tunnel was begun from opposite sides of the hill. Incredibly, when the diggers met

in the middle, their drillings coincided within a few feet. Pythagoras himself was revered in his time and later as an almost mystically intuitive mathematician. Perhaps Polycrates' famous tunnel owed something to a survey made by Pythagoras in youth. But the philosopher disapproved of the tyrant. He followed his fortune westward to freedom, as so many of his adventurous contemporaries were doing. "Greater Greece" was the term in those days for southern Italy and Sicily. Being so much freer, more fertile and open than the homeland, that region stood in somewhat the same relation to Greece as America was to hold for the European continent. Pythagoras chose the city of Croton, on the instep of the Italian boot, for his new home. There is some evidence that he designed the very large and beautiful coins of Croton, which represent no local deity but instead an ear of corn. Like some Protestant missionary in a promised land, Pythagoras proceeded to invent a whole way of life for the citizens of Croton. By all accounts, his followers wore white and ate no meat. The outer circle of devotees practiced trade, politics, and war—all with signal success, at least at first. The inner circle, meanwhile, contemplated the cosmos or universal harmony as it appeared to them in mathematical form. This exer-

A terra-cotta statuette shows a peasant plowing behind a team of oxen.

cise, Pythagoras taught, exalts the soul and draws it toward eternal things. His doctrine appears allied in some way to Indian religion and Orphism. Something of its spirit was to be made manifest again in Plato, Plotinus, and Saint Augustine.

Pythagoras is said to have discovered the laws of intervals in music by means of experiments with blacksmiths' hammers and with bow-strings. Typically, he extended those researches in a metaphysical manner to arrive at what he called "the music of the spheres" in their courses. He was by common consent one of the most influential forces in the whole intellectual history of the West; and yet, not one word from Pythagoras' own lips has reliably come down to us. The trouble is not just that he wrote nothing, but also that he enjoined silence upon his many disciples from generation to generation. This fact in itself, of course, is not without interest. Secrecy appears to have been an inherent element of Pythagorean philosophy. But let us conclude with a cautious and sober summary of Pythagoras' doctrine which was set down by a neo-Platonic philosopher named Porphyry.

"What Pythagoras said to his disciples no man can tell for certain, since they preserved such an exceptional silence. However, the following facts in particular became universally known: first that he held the soul to be immortal, next that it migrates into other kinds of animal, further that past events repeat themselves in a cyclic process and nothing is new in an absolute sense, and finally that one must regard all living things as kindred. These are the beliefs which Pythagoras is said to have been the first to introduce into Greece."

No people in the world has had a history more rich in major thinkers than the Greek. To suppress philosophy or give it second place even in a swift survey such as this would mean distorting what the Greeks have done. By the same token, it would be a serious mistake to point to the great thinkers of the past as having been merely clever enough to anticipate twentieth-century knowledge. They did far more than that, obviously. The questions raised by the earliest Greek philosophers are very much with us still. Why? Because they so often point to loopholes in thought which conventional learning will never close up.

But now the brilliant dawn of classical Greece gives way to lurid sunrise. Very terrible and also glorious struggles await her, as we shall see in the coming chapter.

CHAPTER III

THE
PERSIAN
WAR

Ionia, at the start of the fifth century before Christ, attempted to throw off the yoke which Cyrus' Persians had imposed. Athens and Eretria (a city on the island of Euboea to the northeast of Athens) warmly sympathized with their sister cities on the far side of the Aegean. They sent an expedition to aid their uprising. That force succeeded in razing Sardis, which had once belonged to Croesus and was now a Persian provincial capital. But the revolt as a whole failed utterly; Ionia remained enslaved. Worse, the Persian lion had been aroused to come bounding down upon little Greece.

The next two decades witnessed a most amazing war between East and West. The Greek historian Herodotus was a baby when that began. He grew up to immortalize the struggle in a wonderful account running close to a quarter of a million words. The war was in fact crucial for us all. This brief chapter, therefore, will deal with it alone. But first, one has to ask how far ancient accounts are to be trusted. The labors of archaeologists and classical archivists in our day do bear out many things which were once thought to be sheer legend. Yet even the great Herodotus himself strikes modern readers as credulous—

Athena, goddess of organized warfare, appears in martial attire in this bronze.

even superstitious. One ought, however, to keep in mind the fact that classical movers and shakers held more or less the same beliefs as did Herodotus. It follows that dreams, omens, and oracles had no small influence on actual events. So one may tread Herodotus' footsteps with a certain gingerly confidence after all. His narrative presents, naturally enough, an immensely complex tangle of conflicting interests. Still, its main thread is clear: war to the knife between the greatest despotism ever seen up to that time and a new thing under the sun, a people owing free allegiance to the rule of law.

As Herodotus tells the story, when the emperor Darius was told that Sardis had been sacked, he called for his bow. "Grant, oh God, that I may punish the Athenians!" he cried, and shot an arrow toward the sun. His religion, by the way, was Zoroastrian. Darius worshiped a single deity: Mazda, or "Illumination." In this sense the Persians were more advanced than the Greeks, who still worshiped an entire pantheon of highly personal and even petulant deities. But Persian monotheism was reflected in politics to make Darius seem a sort of God on Earth. He acknowledged neither peers nor subjects, for all people within his reach were looked upon as "slaves" to Darius. Since the Athenians had in effect bitten his hand, he felt obliged to punish them as one might punish a half-wild and forgetful dog, perhaps, on the forest edge of one's great estate. In order to remind himself of this, Darius had his butler repeat the words "Remember the Athenians!" each time dinner was served. He also sent heralds to Athens, and to Sparta as well, demanding "Water and Earth," as called for by Persian custom, in token of submission. At both cities, the Persian heralds were promptly and shamefully put to death. The only excuse the hosts gave for this outrage was that Darius' ambassadors had desecrated the native tongue by making their demand in Greek.

Angered to action, Darius dispatched a fleet of six hundred vessels against Greece. The fleet made a halt at the mid-Aegean island of Delos, which was revered as the birthplace of two Greek deities, Apollo and Artemis. Datis, the Persian commander, probably expected some show of welcome from the islanders, considering the fact that his force outnumbered the entire native population. He found to his surprise that everyone had fled; Delos was deserted. So Datis made a proclamation to the empty air asserting that he had meant the Delians

no harm. By way of sacrifice, he burned a vast amount of frankincense on Apollo's altar. Soon after his departure westward over the horizon, Delos was shaken by an earthquake for the first and only time in recorded history. "It may well be," Herodotus remarks, "that the shock was an act of God to warn men of the troubles that were on the way; for it is true enough that during the three generations comprising the reigns of Darius the son of Hystaspes, and of his son Xerxes and his grandson Artaxerxes, Greece suffered more misery than in the six hundred years before Darius was born—partly from the Persian wars, partly from her own internal struggles for supremacy."

Those miseries began with Datis' destruction of Eretrea. The temples of the town were sacked and burned in reprisal for the burning of Sardis, and the entire population was carried off as prisoners. Datis planned to punish Athens in the same way. He next sailed to the beach of Marathon. Only ten thousand Athenian citizen-soldiers, plus perhaps a thousand allies from the Boeotian town of Plataea, stood between him and Athens. The Persians, who had the reputation of being invincible, outnumbered the defenders at least ten to one. Datis' famed Persian bowmen, rank upon rank in their gaily plumed headdresses, stood ready to becloud the sky with swarms of arrows. The Persian infantry was armed with wicker shields, short spears, and battle-axes. Behind the footmen, to make sure they held the line, were officers cracking bullwhips strong enough to break a neck. A Scythian contingent carrying bows and iron-studded clubs held the Persian center.

The Greeks debated whether to attack this terrifying array or whether to beat a twenty-five-mile retreat to the walls of Athens. The Athenian minister of war cast the deciding vote: attack. Miltiades, the general who had most strongly urged this course, now assumed the supreme command. Thanks to the Greek passion for athletics, rather than to strictly military training, his men were in superb condition. Their main weapons were thrusting spears. Their courage sprang partly from desperation, since every man knew what Eretrea's fate had been. They had no cavalry, and no archers. At Miltiades' signal, the Greeks leveled their spears and started running down the slope toward the Persian host, which stood confidently below, more than a mile off.

Silently the Greeks came on, a thin line of them, gathering momentum all the time, and gaining second wind. When finally they hit, their

spears crashed right on through the wicker shields of the Persians. They bent the Persian line into a V shape, with the Scythians—who held fast—at its apex. The thing happened so fast that the Persian cavalry had nowhere to go. The regiments of Persian archers loosed only a few flights of arrows, for then the Greeks were in amongst them and the battle had begun to roll back like a rattling tide upon the shore. It continued right into the water as the Persians scrambled aboard their ships. Athens captured seven vessels that day, but Datis and the major part of his force got away. Still, when it was over, the Greeks found to their own surprise that they had achieved a decisive victory. As against losses of a mere hundred and ninety-two men on their side, they had slaughtered no less than 6,400 of the enemy. The Persian survivors sailed home, badly mauled. Not for ten years would Asia dare invade Europe a second time.

Sparta, meanwhile, regretted her inhospitality toward the heralds of Darius. Greek and Asiatic custom alike held ambassadors to be sacrosanct. A pair of Spartan warriors therefore volunteered to journey to the court of Darius and offer their own lives as recompense. In the course of this journey they were entertained by a Persian satrap who admired their spirit. "Offer your services to Persia, not your lives," he suggested. "If you do that, you might soon find yourselves in authority over Greek territories which our King would present to you." The Spartans thanked their host for his counsel, but explained, "You know only one half of what is involved in this. The other half remains a blank to you. You understand slavery, but you have never experienced freedom. If you had any idea what freedom really is you would advise us to fight for it not with spears only but with axes as well." Traveling on, they learned that Darius had died in the course of a campaign against the Scythians, and that his son Xerxes now occupied the throne. At the entrance to the royal audience chamber, Xerxes' bodyguards tried to force the warriors to their knees. But the Spartans managed to keep their footing. They informed Xerxes that Greek custom forbade them to worship any mere human being. They had come into his presence for a different purpose. Namely, to offer their lives in reparation for those of the Persian ambassadors to Sparta. Magnanimously, Xerxes replied that he would not dream of repaying one crime with another. Sparta, he added, had broken a law which the whole world held sacred.

Situated on a cliff at Cape Sounion on the tip of Attica, the ruined temple to Poseidon commands a view far out over the Aegean.

The city could not expect to escape the burden of its guilt by offering reprisals in kind. With that, Xerxes sent the two Spartans home again.

The incident rather neatly points up one of the irreconcilable differences which brought Greece and Persia into conflict. The Greek love of freedom was not negotiable. The notion appears first in Homer, who observed that "a slave is only half a man." The Greeks knew that very well for they were, after all, a slave-owning people. Perhaps a quarter to a third of their population in classical times consisted of slaves purchased abroad, or taken in battle, and native-born serfs such as those whom the Spartans kept under heel. The free citizens of the Greek city-states, therefore, had a horror of calling any man "Master." True, they supported "tyrants" of their own at times, in Athens, Samos, Corinth, and elsewhere. But such men ruled on sufferance as it were, and none remained secure. Pisistratus, the tyrant of Athens, for example, was a brilliant and refreshing leader as even his enemies confessed, and yet found himself deposed more than once. His sons carried on the dynasty for a time, but one of them suffered assassination. Harmodius and Aristogeiton, who cut the proud prince down, were in fact honored with a monument. And after that the city practiced radical democracy. Not only did every adult male citizen possess a vote, but all were eligible for constantly rotating public offices chosen by lot. This would have led to chaos in the administration, but for one stabilizing factor: Athenian respect for the rule of law.

The political picture at Sparta was paradoxical also. There, liberty came from just the opposite quarter. Deliberately old-fashioned, Sparta had managed to retain through thick and thin a kind of constitutional monarchy. Real power rested with a council of elders, old soldiers supported by a standing army which comprised the entire adult male citizenry—perhaps eight thousand strong. By rights this should have made for an intolerably unfree society. But just as the Athenians had learned from Solon what a steadying thing is law, so the Spartans had learned from Lycurgus how law can protect individual freedom. Not liberty alone, therefore, but liberty under law was what the Greek people stood ready to defend. Their gods were capricious and cruel, often enough. So were their own leaders now and then, of course. But the Greeks had determined that they would live subject to no man's personal whim alone.

Not long after the Battle of Marathon, the Athenian miners struck an extremely rich vein of silver near Cape Sounion. What was to be done with this new wealth? The question came up in the Assembly. At first, the citizens favored turning it all into coins which would be distributed equally amongst themselves. They were dissuaded by a rising young politician named Themistocles. He quietly pointed out the fact that Athens stood in need of a strong navy to protect her burgeoning international trade. The city now imported grain from Egypt and from colonies on the Black Sea, dried fish from the Bosporus, and timber from Thrace. Her chief exports were olive oil, exquisitely painted pottery, and weapons. Athenian workshops were supplying householders and soldiers throughout most of the Mediterranean world. Yet her navy still consisted of a few obsolete *penteconters*— fifty-oared vessels. Themistocles, therefore, proposed using the silver windfall to build a fleet of modern triremes. By arranging the rowers in three tiers one above the other, power and maneuverability were much increased. A long bronze beak, plowing the water line out front, was the main armament. Themistocles had a private reason for urging the construction of these vessels. He felt certain that the Persians would return to take revenge for their defeat at Marathon. But it did not seem politic, in happy Athens, to make a public issue of danger.

While Themistocles was putting together his navy strange things were happening at Susa, Xerxes' faraway capital. The lord of most of the known world had experienced two terrible dreams in which a phantom commanded him to campaign against Greece. Xerxes' uncle and close adviser, Artabanus, also had a dream from which he gathered that heaven itself was about to send ruin upon Greece. Convinced that these visions were vouchsafed by God, Xerxes set his war machine into motion.

The preparations occupied four full years. King Xerxes intended to take no chances. He levied troops from all his provinces. Their grand total topped five million, according to Herodotus. (Modern historians find this difficult to accept, despite the fact that Herodotus itemized his figures province by province.)

The "Great King and King of Kings," as Xerxes styled himself, marshaled his army at the Hellespont (the modern-day Dardanelles). His engineers had thrown two bridges across the strait, but both were

swept away by the tides. Xerxes had the men in charge decapitated and
the swift-flowing waters of the Hellespont chastised for their intran-
sigence. New bridges made of boats which had been lashed together
were then constructed and Xerxes' polyglot force began its inexorable
march toward the Greek mainland.

When his army reached Abydos, Xerxes sat on a hill to review
the whole mass of his troops drawn up below. The flower of the army
was his personal bodyguard of ten thousand "Immortals," knights in
golden armor. Then too there were Bactrians and Indian archers with
arrows of cane, Ethiopians in lion skins whose arrows were tipped with
flint, Red Sea warriors with crane-skin shields, Libyans carrying fire-
hardened javelins, Thracians in fawn-skin boots and fox-skin headdresses, Pisidians wearing horned helmets and crimson leggings, Caspian horsemen armed with daggers and lassos, and Bedouins mounted
on camels. Anchored nearby offshore, and also under the king's happy
eye, were 1,207 fully manned Egyptian, Phoenician, Syrian, and Cyprian triremes. To entertain the king, the naval contingents staged a
regatta: a rowing match, which the Phoenicians won. Xerxes took as
much delight in this as in the whole fearsome array of his army. It
looked as if his invasion of Greece would be a triumphal procession
rather than a war.

Meanwhile, Xerxes' intended victims were consulting the Delphic
oracle. The Spartans were first to arrive at the shrine and learn of the
horrors in store. They would assuredly lose their freedom or, if not
that, one of their kings. Such was Apollo's prophecy to the Spartans.
Next came the Athenian delegation. Before the Athenians could so
much as open their mouths to ask a question, the inspired priestess of
Apollo screamed a warning of defeat and destruction. The Athenians
retreated in despair. But soon they were back again, as suppliants, with
olive branches in their hands to beg for a better prophecy. They could
never return home, they explained, with what she had already given
them. At this, the oracle seemed to relent somewhat. Apollo now
promised: "Truly a day will come when you will meet him [the host
from Asia] face to face. Divine Salamis, you will bring death to
women's sons when the corn is scattered, or the harvest gathered in."

It is worth pausing here for a moment to ask a question which has
puzzled almost all careful students of the classical world. Was the

Persian archers, clad in exotic Eastern costumes, on a relief of glazed brick

Delphic oracle a fraud, by and large? Or did some genuinely prophetic inspiration play into it? Among the Greeks themselves, Aristotle was one of the first to ponder this. He noted the obvious fact that Delphi practiced a good deal of deliberate ambiguity, so designed as to make the oracle seem right no matter what happened. Also, he pointed out, Apollo exhibited a suspicious vagueness in matters of time. Take for instance the promise that Salamis would "bring death to women's sons when the corn is scattered, or the harvest gathered in." Why should the god have hesitated between spring and fall if, as Delphi claimed, Apollo really *knew*? Delphi's prophecies were such as to excite wonder rather than give confidence. Hundreds of thousands of suppliants, over a period of many centuries, seem to have found the Delphic oracle reliable, which gives one pause at least.

In any case, the oracle's warnings to Sparta and Athens concerning the Persian invasion were well-informed. The constant stream of questioning pilgrims to Delphi kept the priests of the shrine well up on what was going on in the world. Delphi possessed a sort of pilgrim intelligence-gathering system which was unrivaled and indeed unique. The priests in charge at the shrine knew that Xerxes' oncoming host might outnumber the defenders of Greece by a thousand to one. They were also aware of the fact that northeastern Greece was actually aiding the invader. All that being so, Apollo's prophecies were strictly in line with probability. A suitably programed computer would have printed out the same dire warnings, more or less, if a computer could utter poetry. But when the Athenians showed the perseverance to beg for a second oracle, the answer they got went beyond the probable to the truly prophetic. Did someone in the Athenian delegation tip off the priests to the plans which Themistocles had drawn up for the defense of Athens? Themistocles understood that the city could not possibly stand against Xerxes. He was counting on a strategic retreat to the island of Salamis, which he meant to defend with the "wooden wall" he had foresightedly provided—the Athenian navy.

The Delphians themselves asked their oracle what was to be done, and got a brief answer: "Pray to the winds." This might be taken in either of two ways; as serious advice or as an indication that things were hopeless. However, storms did rob Xerxes of approximately half his fleet before the battle had even been joined. It did appear, Herodo-

tus remarks, as if the winds were doing everything they could to whittle the Persian fleet down to size.

The land army of the Great King (a title which Xerxes' successors would also bear) would be entering central Greece by the Pass of Thermopylae: a fifty-foot-wide stretch between a precipitous mountain and the sea. His navy, meanwhile, would be passing down the long narrow channel between the island of Euboea and the mainland. They were due to force both passages at just about the time of the Olympian Games: a holy season for the Greeks, during which war became something of an impiety. Sparta, in particular, refused to let the Persian threat interfere with the games at Olympia. She sent a mere token force of three hundred men to help defend Thermopylae. The rest, Sparta promised, would be along after the games were over. Meanwhile, as a pledge of faith, Leonidas, the king of Sparta, took personal command of the holding action. Leonidas must have had a fair inkling of the trials in store at Thermopylae. He selected none but middle-aged veterans to go with him. Each man of his three hundred left at least one son at home to carry on the family name. Also, Leonidas must surely have had somewhere at the back of his mind or in the depths of his heart the words which the Delphic oracle had spoken. Apollo had seemed to imply that Sparta might be saved if one of her kings were to die.

Xerxes drew up his forces at Thermopylae and waited there patiently for a full four days. His scouts informed him that the enemy had built a wall across the pass but that they seemed to be very few in number. Xerxes supposed that they would flee, and save his troops the trouble of storming the wall. But they stayed, and eventually the Persians attacked. To Xerxes' utter disgust, his troops proved to be no match for the Greeks on a man-to-man basis. Day after day, the Persians were bloodily beaten back from the narrow way. Finally, local guides showed Xerxes a steep, secret path over the mountain. Using that route, the invaders got around Thermopylae and prepared to close a trap on its defenders.

As soon as he learned what was afoot, Leonidas hastily dismissed most of his allies—all except the Thebans and the Thespians. He intended Sparta and Sparta alone to have the glory of the battle to come. He and his men did not await the Persian assault but went to meet it.

They did great slaughter by driving masses of invaders to trample each other and drown in the sea. When the Spartan spears were broken, swords came into play. After that, Leonidas and his men fought with fists and teeth until they died.

Thermopylae was one of those heroic failures which infinitely surpass an easy victory in their psychological effect. It amounted to no more than a passing annoyance and momentary frustration, from the Persian viewpoint. But to the Greeks, naturally, Thermopylae became a rallying cry. Meanwhile, the allied Greek fleet rowed out against the Asian enemy as it came. The Greek ships formed a circle in the center of the strait between the mainland and the island of Euboea, with their prows raying outward like the spines of a sea urchin. The Persian navy was vastly superior in numbers and also in speed and seamanship. It was with every confidence of quick success, therefore, that the Asiatic force smartly surrounded the Greek one and converged upon it. Some vessels belonging to Persia's Phoenician allies succeeded in breaking through the Greek circle of bronze-beaked ships, only to find themselves surrounded, and the struggle continued until nightfall. It was resumed in the morning, with the same results as before. On the third day, the losses suffered by both sides were severe. Still, the Greek fleet held firm in its circle. Meanwhile, two hundred triremes which the Persians had dispatched around the outside of Euboea were wrecked in a squall. This news raised the spirits of the Greek allies, but then came word that the Pass of Thermopylae had been forced. Themistocles at once suggested slaughtering all sheep and cattle within reach on the island in order to give the men a feast. This was done. Then the Greeks left their campfires burning, pushed their bloodstained ships into the water, and slipped off to the south with muffled oars.

Athens lay empty, awaiting the invader. Just a few religious fanatics and down-and-out citizens had elected to defend the Acropolis to the last. They crowned the citadel with a flimsy barricade of uprooted fences and broken furniture. This, they told each other, was really the "wooden wall" to which the Delphic oracle had referred. And indeed, it did give Xerxes' troops some little trouble. But Persian archers managed to burn sections of the barricade by shooting flaming arrows up into it. Then the Acropolis was overwhelmed and its defenders killed. The Great King himself arrived. Master of a silent and dead

A griffon head, cast in bronze at Olympia in the mid-seventh century B.C.

city, he ordered everything burned to the ground. The smoke of Athens drifted southwestward to darken the offshore island of Salamis.

The Athenians, with their movable possessions, were encamped on the island. Only a narrow stretch of water and the Greek fleet of some three hundred and eighty ships stood between them and destruction. Worse, Athens' allies were threatening to pull out. Eurybiades, the Spartan commander, favored making a stand at the isthmus of Corinth and letting Salamis go by default. Themistocles bitterly opposed that suggestion, of course, but he was a minority of one in the allied war council. When he tried to speak, the Corinthian commander raised an objection: "Why should we waste our time listening to Themistocles? He's a man without a country now." Enraged, Themistocles threatened to abandon the whole war. He could easily win a new country for Athens—perhaps in Italy—with his two hundred ships. The other commanders recognized the truth of that. In order to keep Themistocles and his ships, they agreed to hold firm in the Strait of Salamis.

Themistocles, however, suspected that it was only a question of time before the Peloponnesian elements of the navy would break and sail for home. Therefore he confided in a trusted slave named Sicinnus who had attended his children, and asked the man to somehow reach Xerxes with a message. Sicinnus succeeded, carrying the intelligence that he was "the bearer of secret communications from the Athenian commander, who is a well-wisher to your king and hopes for a Persian victory. He has told me to report to you that the Greeks have no confidence in themselves and are planning to save their skins by a hasty withdrawal. Only prevent them from slipping through your fingers, and you have at this moment an opportunity of unparalleled success. They are at daggers drawn with each other, and will offer no opposition—on the contrary you will see the pro-Persians amongst them fighting the rest." The message made sense to Xerxes; the Great King was taken in. That same evening, his navy sailed out to block the strait at both ends and prevent the Greeks from slipping away during the night. Xerxes ordered a crushing attack for the next morning. He would personally be watching the whole engagement. A marble throne was set up for him upon a ridge overlooking the strait. Being under his own eye, the Asiatic navy would perform splendidly—much better than it had at Artemision, Xerxes assumed.

The Greek forces meanwhile, unaware of what lay in store, slept well. Awakening at sunrise to find their ships bottled up, the Greeks assembled on shore and sang a paean to their gods. The music of their singing carried to the Persian ships which had already begun crowding into the strait. Themistocles briefly addressed the men. The fate of Greece would be determined by their courage during the day ahead. He gave the order to embark. The Greek ships very shortly began smashing their bronze beaks into the flank of the oncoming armada. The narrowness of the strait afforded small room for maneuver. Hand-to-hand combat raged across the decks of wallowing and sinking ships. The Greek vessels were the sturdiest on the whole, and each Greek marine did the work of ten. The oars of most ships were sheared off in the crush. Greek oarsmen used the splintered stumps left in their hands as weapons. Wreckage, the drowning, and the already slain spun round and round together in the bloody surge. At sunset, what little remained of the Asiatic fleet drew back from the strait. Xerxes, weeping, stepped down from his throne to order the execution of various captains.

His immense army had suffered no reverse; it still could dominate Greece. But Xerxes' navy was largely gone beneath the waves at Salamis. Lacking ships, he could not keep his army supplied for long. His millions of troops would starve for lack of provisions and would become prey for the Greeks whom Xerxes had intended to enslave. The Great King himself might be taken captive, or killed in battle on Greek soil. He had his huge empire to think about. And so, Xerxes decided to get out of Greece fast. He was afraid his enemies might sail to destroy his bridges over the Hellespont, thereby cutting off all retreat. Themistocles was in fact urging just such a course.

But another brilliant Athenian leader, Aristides, pointed out that Xerxes would be all the more dangerous if he were trapped in Europe. Themistocles, finding himself overruled, sent Sicinnus once again with a message to the Great King. "I have come on behalf of the commander of the Athenian fleet," Sicinnus told Xerxes. "Themistocles is still doing all he can to serve your interests. He has managed to dissuade the Greeks from pursuing the remnants of your fleet and going on to destroy your bridges across the Hellespont. He wishes you to reach Asia without interference." This time, too, Xerxes welcomed Themistocles' message. Hastily, he began his long march home. His army, which had

OVERLEAF: *A vase painting portrays physically fit Greek athletes competing with one another in a spirited foot race.*

done hardly any fighting whatsoever, did suffer terribly from hunger on the return journey. Eating whatever they could find, down to bits of leather and tree bark, the troops were decimated by dysentery. Of those who reached Asia Minor, thousands stuffed themselves with too much food too suddenly, and died in the midst of plenty.

A distinguished Persian general named Mardonius had received Xerxes' permission to remain behind in Greece. He claimed that with three hundred thousand picked troops, he would deliver Greece in chains to the Great King. He planned to winter in Thessaly, and conquer Greece the following spring. With the beginning of hostilities, he made the strong fortress of Thebes his base. Being hereditary enemies of Athens, the Thebans made Mardonius and his troops very welcome. The war was not over yet. One climactic battle of a very strange, albeit heroic, sort had yet to be fought.

King Alexander of Macedon (a forebear of Alexander the Great) joined with the Thebans in promoting the Persian cause. He himself journeyed to Athens and spoke to the victorious Assembly there amongst the ruins. "Mardonius has sent me," he said, "to let you know that if only you submit Xerxes will rebuild your city and your temples and furthermore grant you free dominion over other Greek territories. The Great King's offer to forget the past and be your friend honors you very much, and I personally urge that you accept it. Should you fail to do so, Attica must remain a no-man's-land lying between the invincible Mardonius and your impotent Peloponnesian allies." Spartan envoys spoke next to the Assembly, exhorting the Athenians to stand firm. Then the Athenians gave their answer, which Herodotus records as follows: "So long as the sun keeps its present course in the sky, we Athenians will never make peace with Xerxes. On the contrary, we shall oppose him unremittingly, putting our trust in the help of the gods and heroes whom he despised, whose temples and statues he detroyed with fire."

As soon as those words were reported back to Mardonius at Thessaly, the Persian general made ready to lay waste Athens' territories anew. Spring—fighting weather—had come. The leading men of Thessaly argued that Mardonius could best bring about the downfall of Greece by using bribes to detach the city-states one by one from their common cause. But Mardonius wanted action. Marching south, he re-

captured Athens. It was deserted; again the citizens had fled to Salamis.
Mardonius sent heralds across to the island, repeating the proposal
which Alexander had made. It was rejected a second time, and the only
Athenian who dared suggest a debate on the matter was lynched
with all his family. Meanwhile, Athenian envoys were at Sparta beg-
ging for help. "Put your army in the field," they insisted. "Your hesita-
tion is unworthy of the hour and of yourselves." The Spartans would
make no immediate reply. There was a holy festival going on at the
time, a traditional excuse for not fielding troops.

If Athens was the wily Odysseus of the free Greek world, Sparta
was mighty Ajax, carrying the heaviest shield—a magnificent standing
army. Of course it was partly due to their policy of advancing only
when necessary, that the Spartans had a reputation for never retreating
in war. Besides, every battle of a major sort that Sparta fought put her
in double jeopardy; because defeat in the field could so easily spark a
revolt amongst the Helots and Messenians at home. For reasons such as
these the Spartans kept putting off an answer to their Athenian friends.
At last the envoys were reduced to using threats. Suppose that Athens
were to accept Mardonius' terms, they said, then what would happen
to Sparta? The balance of power in Greece would tip against the
Peloponnesus, in such a case. The Spartans grasped the frightening
logic of this. At long last, they dispatched a force of five thousand
superb fighters: heavily armed hoplites, each one of them supported
by no less than seven light-armed Helots.

Learning of the allied Greeks' advance, Mardonius withdrew his
men to the Boeotian plain in order to be near the walls of Thebes in
the unlikely event of a setback. Mardonius possessed perhaps three
times as many troops (including his own Greek allies) as the free
Greek force of 110,000 soldiers. The opposing armies faced each other
in the territory of Platea. Soothsayers on both sides warned against attack. So both forces declined to begin full-scale hostilities. For more
than a week, nothing was accomplished except by the Persian cavalry,
which harassed the allied troops with hit-and-run archery attacks and
succeeded in fouling their water supply. The Spartan wing of the allied
army held the position of honor facing Mardonius' own Immortals.
The Athenians, at the far end of the line, opposed their ancient
enemies, the Thebans. But now the Spartan general, Pausanius, sug-

gested a switch. After all, he said, the Athenians were more familiar with Persian tactics. They had overcome at Marathon. So the Spartan and Athenian troops changed places. Mardonius, observing the maneuver, switched his own wings as well; and then he sent a herald to the Spartan lines. "Men of Lacedaemon," his message ran, "everyone around here seems to think you are very brave. You stick to your posts, they say, until death. But this is obviously nonsense, for we find you stealing away from us as timidly as deer—with not even a blow struck. Hold still. We challenge you. Let us do combat, Persians against Spartans, the champions of Asia against the champions of Greece. Let there be equal numbers on both sides, and let our battle decide the whole conflict." Pausanius and his Spartans made no response.

That night, under cover of darkness, the allied Greek army began to retreat toward higher ground near to a potable spring. They never made it, however. Dawn found the slow-moving Spartans only half way to their new position. Gleefully, the hand-picked Persians of Mardonius pursued and fell upon them. The Thebans meanwhile cut off the Athenian retreat in a running battle. The center of the free Greek force had fallen further back and therefore played no part in the initial stages of the day's struggle. The Athenians, for their part, gradually gained the upper hand against the attacking Thebans. The Spartans meanwhile stood and suffered stoically under swarms of Persian arrows, until at last Pausanius gave the order to charge. In the close work that followed, they were magnificent. Man against man, they utterly outfought the bravest and best warriors of the East. Mardonius, riding a white charger, was struck down. Thereupon the battle turned into a rout. The Greek center, with the Athenians, came up in time to destroy the remaining Persians. Not one invader in a hundred survived. Greek freedom was finally assured. Not Athenian generalship, this time, but Spartan spears had carried most of the burden.

Almost in the moment of triumph, however, came the beginnings of a dissension which would eventually rip Greece in half. Athens set to work to rebuild her walls from the rubble that Xerxes and Mardonius had left. But Sparta objected. Now that Greece was safe again, the Spartans said, such fortifications were not needed. To rebuild them now would be to show distrust and disrespect for one's Greek allies. Themistocles, taking a leaf from the Spartans' own book, temporized

A Spartan warrior, cast in bronze, wears a body-concealing cloak and helmet.

and gave deliberately vague answers until the walls had risen to a formidable state. Then he bluntly informed Sparta that Athens was quite capable of deciding her own affairs.

Themistocles informed the Athenian Assembly that he had a suggestion to make which would immensely benefit Athens but which could not be discussed publicly. It was one of those awkward moments met with in the practice of democracy. How are people to vote on things which require secrecy? The solution hit upon in this case was ingenious. The people directed Themistocles to confide his stratagem to one man alone. The person selected was Aristides—the same man who had frustrated Themistocles' previous plan to destroy Xerxes' bridge of ships across the Hellespont. The citizens called him Aristides the Just. He had distinguished himself in battle three times over: at Marathon, at Salamis, and at Plataea. Reluctantly, Themistocles bent down and whispered a few words in his rival's ear. Aristides nodded to show that he understood. Then, rising, he proclaimed: "To carry out this secret proposal would indeed be to our advantage, most extraordinarily so. But it would also be despicable!"

The matter ended there. Not until years later did Themistocles' scheme become known. The whole allied Greek fleet had been based at that moment in Athenian territory, and Themistocles had counseled burning it, as if by accident. That would have given Athens, with its strong trireme-building program, command of the continuing Greek struggle to sweep Persia from the Aegean Sea.

But Athens led that struggle without such treachery, thanks to the generalship of Aristides, and to Themistocles' diplomacy. In the course of the next few years, the allied fleet won victory after victory. Freedom was restored to the islands and Ionia. Themistocles made a habit of exacting heavy "contributions" from those who were freed.

Slander said that much of what Themistocles collected stuck to his own fingers, and perhaps it did. In any case, there were no libel laws, and the leaders of democratic Athens found themselves regularly pilloried by part-humorous and part-vicious accusations. Envy seems to have been a major vice of Athens in her happiest days. Banishment of the great became a common thing. Themistocles himself was one of the first to suffer it. Under attack for avarice, he departed Athens and went to live in the city-state of Argos. But now more solemn

charges were leveled against him. Themistocles stood accused of having communicated treasonously with Xerxes. Athenian agents were sent to snatch him home for trial. Themistocles escaped his pursuers, just barely, by traveling northward into barbarous Epirus. Incognito, and by a circuitous route, he made his way at last to the Persian Court.

Xerxes was dead. Artaxerxes, his son, occupied the throne. Themistocles, ever supple, went before the young Great King. "I did everything I could to help your father," he lied, "and now I have come to offer you, also, my devotion." Artaxerxes was pleased. "Begin," he commanded, "by telling me all you can about your country." Themistocles demurred, for the moment. A mind, he explained, is like a carpet which must be unrolled all the way before its true pattern becomes apparent. He begged for a year in which to learn the Persian tongue and marshal all his thoughts for the Great King. Again, Artaxerxes gave consent. The king learned to cherish Themistocles over the years. The strategist and statesman who had saved the West ended his days as a grand vizier in the East. It is said that he raised a new family in old age, and named his favorite daughter "Asia." And yet by virtue of Themistocles' own genius, the future now lay with Greece.

CHAPTER IV

THE
EDUCATION
OF HELLAS

Well before the middle of the fifth century B.C., Athens ceased
to be a champion of Greek freedom. Having chased the Persians from
Aegean waters, and having liberated Ionia, she now became empress
of maritime Greece. Athenian galleys made a grand tour every year,
collecting protection money from a dozen or more erstwhile allies. The
fiction that they still formed a defensive "league" was carefully maintained. But in fact defections from the league were ruthlessly punished
by Athenian seapower. The league treasury was moved from the sacred
island of Delos to Athens, and Athenians alone kept its account books.
Island coinage gradually was suppressed in favor of the Athenian
mint. All political and business disputes of importance within the
league were referred automatically to Athenian courts. Athenian sailors and marines made far-flung war their trade. One memorial tablet,
which appears to date from the year 449 B.C., lists 177 men from a
single regiment who died "in Cyprus, in Egypt, in Phoenicia, at
Halaesis, in Aegina, and at Megara—*all in the same year.*"

The chief power in Athens had passed from Aristides the Just to an
aristocratic man of war named Cimon. He was the son of Miltiades, the

Pericles, energetic empire- and metropolis-builder during Athens' Golden Age

hero of Marathon, and an enormously rich, openhanded person. Cimon's dinner table welcomed whomever cared to come. He himself would drink deep with his guests, and sometimes entertain them with a song or two. Themistocles had boasted that although he did not know how to play the harp or sing a song he could raise up a city to greatness. Cimon's friends bragged that their man went Themistocles one better, since he did know how to entertain. Perhaps the new leader's most popular move was to have all the fences around his estates removed, and notices posted inviting the public to come in and pick whatever fruit happened to be in season. Cimon's reputation suffered, nevertheless, and he was accused of being incestuous, pro-Spartan, and a drunkard. But lazy he could not fairly be called. He campaigned at sea year after year and died in the course of an attack on Cyprus.

Cimon's death cleared the way at Athens for a much greater man— Pericles was his name—who was to be credited with nurturing the full blossoming of Athens. Yet, after the wiles of Themistocles, the legendary probity of Aristides, and the bluff splendor of Cimon, Pericles seems oddly flat. The reason may be that he was extraordinarily self-contained. Pericles used to pray that when he rose to speak in the Assembly he would say not one word beside the point. He made a habit of addressing the Assembly on major issues only. Brevity, grace, and logic were his stock in trade. Throughout his whole political career he remained aloof from friend and foe alike. He never dined out; indeed, he never walked in any street except the one which led from his home to the agora and the council chamber. Abuse from his political opponents bothered him not in the least.

He appeared cold, yet it was said that he always greeted his mistress with a kiss. She was a former courtesan named Aspasia, thirty years younger than himself, and a cynosure of the best minds in town. Aspasia kept a salon which used to be attended by such men of genius as Euripides and Socrates. Rumor had it that she wrote Pericles' speeches. Aspasia was doubtless the strongest single influence on his life. The fact that women were not citizens, not politically free, compelled her to work behind the scenes. Yet despite all her discretion, she was brought to trial on the charge of impiety and indecency. Pericles himself won her acquittal by means of a rare show of emotion: he wept before the jurors while pleading Aspasia's case.

Next to Aspasia, the person whom Pericles most admired was the philosopher Anaxagoras. His enemies tried to bring down Anaxagoras also in hopes of destroying Pericles. The philosopher had dared say that he felt more at home in the night sky than in Athens. To some proud patriots, that sounded rather like treason. Worse yet, perhaps, Anaxagoras maintained that the sun was not exactly a divinity but more like a mass of burning rock the size of the Peloponnesus. "Impiety!" cried his accusers. For a while, Pericles managed to protect Anaxagoras, too. However, there came a time when the statesman seemed to forget his wise old friend's existence. Anaxagoras, having no descendants and no means of support, took to his bed and covered up his face with the bedclothes. He was intending to die as quietly as he could. Pericles, hearing of this at last, ran to the philosopher's bedside and entreated him to go on living. He said that he did not lament the fate of Anaxagoras himself so much as he did his own. To lose such a sage counselor would be dreadful. Anaxagoras listened in silence for a while. Finally, he unmuffled his head and said: "Well, Pericles, even a lamp has oil put into it by those who need it."

Since Pericles chose power as against possessions, he could not afford to be generous. He lived within his own small inheritance and never increased it at public expense. He feared scandal, as well he might, and made a point of always deserving his reputation for incorruptibility. But Pericles' public use of the funds which flowed into Athens from its maritime empire was something else again. Never did any city in the history of the world adorn itself so splendidly as Athens under Pericles. His political opponents raged at his building program. Vainglorious, they called it, and perhaps it really seemed to them a comedown from the days of the great sea campaigns under Cimon and Aristides the Just. But sea power was not enough for him. Pericles wished his city to be, in his own phrase, "the education of Hellas." And, thanks very largely to him, Athens became just that.

Sculpture, architecture, drama, and philosophy all flourished wondrously at Athens during the thirty years of Pericles' leadership there. These great feats were achieved not by mere decree, however. Thucydides the historian described Pericles' administration as having been "Democracy in name, but in practice government by the first citizen." Pericles cherished democratic process at Athens, and he was assiduous

in putting public matters to the vote. If his dominance was almost total, still he had to renew it constantly by his powers of persuasion. There came a moment, for example, when he himself felt compelled to ask the Assembly whether or not Athens was spending too much money on public works. "Far too much!" the citizens shouted. "Very well," Pericles responded when silence had been restored. "Do not let it be charged to the public account but to my own, and I will dedicate all the public buildings in my name." This grand gesture raised a second uproar. Everyone present, suddenly, seemed to wish for a share in the glory of what was being done. So the Assembly reversed itself and authorized Pericles to draw whatever was needed from the treasury after all. Pericles thereupon pressed for the banishment of those who had most vociferously objected to his programs. Again, the votes went overwhelmingly his way, and some of his most powerful opponents were run out of town.

Pericles knew how to sway a multitude, and, on top of that, to calculate its motions precisely. He was the primal genius in a brand-new field of human endeavor, a field with an incalculably fabulous future: democratic politics. He knew what wonders can be accomplished by many people working together in one spirit. Equally, he understood how invaluable one single artist may prove to be. Superbly cool himself, he could admire and cherish the fire in the heart of such a person as the sculptor Phidias. Perhaps Pericles' most fruitful inspiration, from the vantage of history, was to set Phidias firmly in charge of Athens' entire building program.

In so swift a chronicle as this there seems almost no place for the nameless creators of the Athens Museum's bearded "Zeus" or "Poseidon," the bronze "Charioteer" at Delphi, or the Olympia pediments. Phidias may have surpassed those masterpieces which were produced in the generation before his own. But they happened to survive, as his own work did not. Mankind possesses less than a hundredth part of the sculptures created in classical Greece. Such revered masters as Phidias and Polycleitus of Argos after him, fared worse in the long run than humbler artisans. Clay figurines, broken carvings, and a few small bronzes might last, but monumental works in ivory, gold, and other precious materials stood no chance at all against the rapacity of man. Nor have the great works of painting by Polygnotus, Zeuxis, and

This elegantly robed and poised charioteer originally belonged to a life-size group, cast at Delphi in the fifth century B.C.

others which once adorned a gallery on the Acropolis, survived. We can only cherish the popular art of the period which has come down to us in the form of vase paintings. But let us enjoy what we can. If all things perish, some of them perish slowly indeed. The Acropolis buildings, which sprang into being during the high summer of Pericles' administration, seem young still—even in ruin.

Phidias undertook to crown the sacred eminence of rock with a new temple for Athena, patroness of Athens, to be called the Parthenon. He also supervised the reconstruction of the Erectheum and the building of a massive Propylaea, or sacred gateway, complete with picture gallery. The two great statues of Athena which once dominated the Acropolis were done by his own hand. The bare rock of the Acropolis itself was, to a sculptor's eyes, already a kind of sculpture; and the buildings done under his direction work together, even today, with the stone and the sky, and even with the distant mountains, in a harmonious relationship which has few peers anywhere. Phidias' vision takes nothing away from the achievement of the architects Ictinus and Callicrates in designing the crowning glory which is the Parthenon. That building occupies a very special place in the mind's eye of almost every visitor to Greece. Its severe Doric order, and the absolute unity of its composition, do not oppress one's soul for a moment. Rather, the Parthenon appears light and alive.

All the long lines of the Parthenon curve just a bit, to bring them into harmony with the curve of the human retina. If the temple foundation lacked a barely perceptible rise in the center, for example (a fact which may be tested by sighting along the floor at eye level), it might appear to sag a little. Again, the columns might look splayed out toward the top if they were not in fact leaning inward slightly, each column itself swelling a bit near mid-height to appear truly straight. The Parthenon is also blessed with an exciting diversity in its unity, owing to the fact that many separate contractors were charged with working on the temple. Each column differs in some small way from its neighbors, for instance, like the trees of a pine forest. This queen of all temples drives surveyors crazy, of course. Nothing about it quite fits a mathematical grid. The total effect infinitely exceeds any possible sum of the Parthenon's separate parts, and beauty such as this is, finally, not subject to analysis.

The bulk of the Parthenon's surviving sculptures may be seen in the British Museum. They appear to have been carved in marble from clay maquettes, so fluid are they. Phidias himself may first have sketched these elements which were, like everything on the Acropolis, done under his personal direction. But the principle figure of Athena, which Phidias put together for the Parthenon's interior, has been lost. She once loomed close to forty feet high within its precincts. Phidias formed white flesh of polished ivory sections invisibly joined. Her yellow-gold tunic must have gleamed like liquid sunlight in the obscurity. At Pericles' suggestion, the gold was bolted into place, fold upon fold. It weighed more than a ton. The time came, as Pericles had foreseen, when Phidias stood accused of retaining some of the gold for his own use. So, upon Pericles' order, the gleaming folds were unbolted and weighed, and not found wanting after all.

The second colossal Athena which Phidias created for the Acropolis stood outdoors. It showed her as defender of the city, armed, with her spear point glittering sixty feet above the rock. The sun sparkled on the polished bronze of this figure, making it visible from far out at sea, like some ancient Statue of Liberty. The Virgin Goddess has gone forever; yet she remains as a sort of inspiration or vision upon the air.

Somewhat the same thing holds true for ancient poetry. At least 90 per cent of the tragedies written by Aeschylus, who flourished in Periclean Athens, are forever lost to us. Yet what little we still possess from his pen carries echoes that are boundless. Simonides and Pindar, who were his contemporaries, left even less to the modern age; but some of their work too is unforgettable. Consider for example Pindar's exclamation of prayer for the contestants in a foot race: "Grant them with feet so light to pass through life!" Or take Simonides' inscription honoring the Spartan dead at Thermopylae:

> *Go tell the Spartans, thou who passest by,*
> *That here obedient to their laws we lie.*

Simonides' naturalness was what made him the all-time master of epigrammatic verse, although in English he sounds uprooted and artificial. As for Pindar's famous odes to the winners of athletic contests, they are like fruity bubbling wines which go sour when shipped any distance at all. The Greek tragedians such as Aeschylus fare only a

OVERLEAF: *Architectural masterpieces, erected in the Doric and Ionic styles atop the ancient Acropolis in Athens between 447* B.C. *and the end of the century*

shade better in translation. To test this out, simply thumb through the best compendium extant: *The Oxford Book of Greek Verse in Translation.* You can easily tell the translators apart from their styles; but can you also, without peeking, distinguish their originals?

Aeschylus himself may be more readily recognized by the dark and splendid tenor of his thought than by his tone of voice. He believed in the Furies. More to the point, he believed that Athens should honor them. "Holy dread," he makes the goddess Athena say in the *Eumenides,* is not to be cast out of the city: "For who among mortals that fears nothing practices justice?"

Not long after Athens' great naval victory at Salamis, Aeschylus celebrated the event as an unmitigated disaster. How was this possible? The answer is simple and startling: he wrote *The Persians* from the Persians' own point of view. Xerxes is the "hero," if such there be, of this well-nigh overwhelming tragedy. Aeschylus treated the whole subject with a thrilling sense of pride for the Greek victory mingled with the most acute and painful awareness of the human condition which is the same for everyone. He has his Persian chorus of mourners sing these verses concerning the Greeks:

> *They pay no more tribute; they bow them no more!*
> *The word of power is not spoken*
> *By the princes of Persia; their day is o'er,*
> *And the laws of the Medes are broken*
> *Through Asia's myriad-peopled land;*
> *For the staff is snapped in the King's right hand.*
>
> *And a watch is not set on the free, frank tongue.*
> *Yea, liberty's voice speaks loud;*
> *And the yoke is loosed from the neck that was wrung*
> *And the back to dominion bowed:*
> *For the earth of Ajax' isle is red*
> *With the blood of Persia's noble dead.*

Aeschylus' Xerxes had felt that there was justification in the heavy yoke which his dominion set upon most of the known world, in order to accomplish great things. Pericles, as leader of Athens, arrived at a not very different notion. Pericles' own voice was not so much frank and free as it was persuasive and skilled in controversy. As for the voice

of Athens herself under Pericles' direction, that became a popular roar,
a mighty shout of a sometimes bloodcurdling kind. The islands and
Ionian city-states which were now subject to Athenian dominion lived
in dread of Athens' navy. No longer were Athenian citizens a small
body of enthusiastic athletes ready to defend their liberty with their
spears as had been done at Marathon. No longer were they the clumsy
but indomitable oarsmen and awesome marines who fought at Salamis.
Athenians now waged harsh and deliberate war in distant places to
extend their city's power. Their oarsmen were highly paid and highly
skilled mercenaries. Their new ships were sleek, sharp, and capable of
intricate maneuvers against enemy vessels. For example, a favorite
Athenian battle trick was to veer suddenly alongside an enemy ship
while retracting oars at the same instant, and thus shear off half the
opponent's oars. That sort of thing required steely nerve and profes-
sionalism. Straightforward courage such as that which Aeschylus and
his comrades had exercised in their youth was no longer enough. In
melancholy fact, Athens' new warriors fought not for freedom but
simply to make their city great. So the plain and objective virtues which
had been the foundation stones of drama in Aeschylus no longer held.
He died disappointed, it is said, in Sicily in the year 456 B.C. The
epitaph on his tombstone made no mention of his immortal contribution to dramatic literature, but simply stated that he had taken a courageous part in the Battle of Marathon. The frank and free tongue, the
voice of liberty, which he had extolled, was becoming something else
by mid-century.

A new master of tragedy, a young man, less inspired perhaps but
more controlled than Aeschylus, now dominated the Athenian stage.
Sophocles was his name. In youth he had been an accomplished singer
and dancer, famous for his good looks. At age sixteen, he was chosen
to lead the chorus in the victory celebrations after the Battle of Salamis. In his early twenties he produced his first tragedies, with instant
success. He himself used to take female roles in his early plays. In middle life he served as Athens' imperial treasurer, and also as general in
a campaign which Pericles undertook for the subjugation of Samos.
On that occasion, according to one anecdote of the period, Sophocles
happened to make a lascivious remark regarding the beauty of a
Samian boy. Thereupon Pericles chided him with the comment that a

commander must constantly strive to keep not only his hands but also his mind clean.

This anecdote raises the vexed question of homosexuality in classical times. The Athenians were both more and less permissive than we. They thought that girls should be virginal until marriage and faithful to their husbands forever after. Boys, on the other hand, were encouraged to develop strong friendships which might indeed become overtly sexual, and occasionally to accept older men as comrades. Greek custom did not lead to homosexuality so much as to male bisexuality. Every man was normally expected to marry. As Pericles himself put the case: "It is impossible for a man to put forward fair and honest views about our affairs if he has not, like everyone else, children whose lives may be at stake." The literary precedent for profound soldierly comradeship best known to every Greek was Homer's account of Achilles and Patroclus. Homer himself, however, gives no indication that their love was physical. The historic precedent for the same thing in the mind of every Athenian was the declared passion between Harmodius and Aristogiton: the young men honored as heroes for having struck down Hipparchus, tyrant of Athens and a son of Pisistratus. There was, finally, a mythical precedent given by Zeus himself. The Father of the Gods condescended to seduce beautiful Prince Ganymede of Troy. But Zeus also begot a large family of gods and demigods in the ordinary way.

That point raises another question which troubles students of Periclean Athens. What part did Olympian religion play in the cultural life of the city? Could anyone so wide-awake as the playwright Sophocles, for instance, really have believed in the gods? This seems difficult to credit, on the face of it. Herodotus, who was one of Sophocles' friends, flatly stated that Homer and Hesiod "made the Greek religion, and distributed to the gods their titles and honors and crafts, and described what they were like." If that statement has any philosophical implication at all it is that men, poets especially, create the gods, and not the reverse. But intellectual belief, emotional faith, and public observance of religion are three different things. In civilized society, at least, these three seldom exhibit any real unity. It is no wonder that we find ourselves perplexed by pagan religion. Will historians two thousand years from now have a prayer of comprehending present-day Christianity?

The playwright Menander, depicted with masks from his comedy, The Curmudgeon

Tragic drama in Athens mainly concerned religion. That much we can say for sure. Its audiences may have been superstitious, and yet at the same time they were the very best for which a serious playwright could wish. Pericles had seen to it that the Athenian poor, far from buying tickets, were paid to attend the theater. They came therefore not as mere passive purchasers of entertainment but as participants in the mind: silent witnesses to a religious and philosophical outpouring. Modern audiences possess millions of snippets of information on thousands of subjects. Contrastingly, Athenian theatergoers in the time of Pericles knew a great deal more than we do about a much smaller range of experience. Their own mythology was in their bones, of course. They could more or less guess in advance how any tragedy based on Greek myth would go. The suspense inherent in such plays was not of the "what happens next?" variety. "*How* will it happen?" That was the question. How is the relatively eternal world of myth to play into this present hour this time around? The particular genius of Sophocles made that question important. His plays poked through time to another dimension, and that remains the most uncanny thing about them even today. They show the gods, in whom his heart surely believed, at work; that is to say, turning the world and shaping the destinies of mankind. As an example of this richly disturbing and portentous quality in Sophocles, listen for just a moment with your inner ear to his evocation of Aphrodite, the Goddess of Love (the translation is mainly by Sir Richard Livingstone):

> *My children, know Love is not Love alone,*
> *But in her name lie many names concealed:*
> *For she is Death, imperishable Force,*
> *Desire unmixed, wild Frenzy, Lamentation:*
> *In her are summed all impulses that drive*
> *To Violence, Energy, Tranquillity.*
> *Deep in each living breast the Goddess sinks,*
> *And all become her prey; the tribes that swim,*
> *The fourfoot tribes that pace upon the earth,*
> *Harbour her; and in birds her wing is sovereign,*
> *In beasts, in mortal men, in gods above.*
> *What god but wrestles with her and is thrown?*

If I may tell—and truth is right to tell—
She rules the heart of Zeus without a spear,
Without a sword. Truly the Cyprian
Shatters all purposes of men and gods.

One tends to think, sometimes, of "ancient" masters of literature as wearing long gray beards and looking terribly severe. This puts them at a disadvantage, for us, and makes them far more difficult to read with sympathy. Sophocles was only a man, after all. The poet Ion, who met him in the course of the campaign against Samos, remarked that the tragedian was "merry and clever over his cups," and that he "seemed to know about as much as the average educated Athenian."

Sophocles lived and reigned as Athens' leading playwright for a very long time. His house held a chapel dedicated to Asclepius, the God of Medicine, and his own person grew in serenity from decade to decade. In old age he was appointed one of ten commissioners to sort out some of the worst wreckage of the Peloponnesian War. Soon after that, it is said, he started a romance with a young courtesan named Theoris. One of Sophocles' sons, fearing for the family estate, thereupon asked an Athenian jury to declare him senile. To refute that charge, Sophocles read out before the court some passages from the tragedy upon which he was then engaged. This was *Oedipus at Colonus,* surely the most magical of all his plays. The passages which the Athenian jury heard were sufficient to convince the court of Sophocles' sanity. At age ninety he attended the funeral of his chief rival, Euripides, and died soon afterward.

Euripides, who was born about the time of the Battle of Salamis, is one of the best known and most problematical authors in all Greek literature. We still possess eighteen plays unquestionably of his authorship, as against seven each from Aeschylus and Sophocles. But Euripides was comparatively "uneven" as the critics say. With his peers one feels safe in a way; one understands more or less what the tone of a tragedy by Aeschylus or Sophocles will be. Not so in the case of Euripides. He was wildly imaginative, probingly sceptical, romantic, and religious by turns. Like ourselves, it seems, Athenian audiences hardly knew what to make of Euripides. He kept producing plays for their dramatic festivals over a period of fifty years, and yet in all that time

his tragedies were awarded only four first prizes. Later generations, however, admired Euripides above the other two masters of tragedy. That is probably the reason why more of his plays than theirs have been preserved. He struck a personal note, habitually, and changed its key from play to play. He made people think along unexpected lines, individually. In his time it was generally held that Athens, the state herself, ought to hold the principal and unchallenged place in the order of human events. So Euripides' contrary view must have been disturbing to many citizens. He distrusted the state and he abhorred Athens' long suicidal war with Sparta. Other playwrights chose kingly heroes and showed them destroyed by divine command—like atoms in an atom smasher. Euripides' tragedies are just as painful as theirs, but not nearly so simple. Not content with bringing down the great, he also exalted the humble; and that was new. The true hero of his *Electra,* for example, is the upright peasant. His heroines were often untried girls and virgin martyrs who displayed a dazzling array of dramatic possibilities. They were nearly consistent, indeed, in violating the canons of "consistency of character" laid down by Aristotle and his like. Euripides cared more for the dragonfly-turns of the human heart, so devious and childish at the same time, than for noble abstraction. Like Socrates, he saw the confusion which underlies most professed principles. (He was, not incidentally, a personal friend of the philosopher.) The same ironically probing and cleansing technique which Socrates performed in conversation dominates Euripidean drama. No wonder that Euripides was less than popular. He is said to have shunned companionship and stayed outside the city as much as he could, usually retreating to a sea cave on the island of Salamis.

Euripides was the first Greek, according to ancient report, who amassed a private library. True or not, that sidelight illuminates once again his furrowed brow and questing mind. In old age he exiled himself to Macedon. It cannot have been an easy move; doubtless he was pushed. But King Archelaus, his Macedonian host, was no savage. The Macedonian court welcomed some old friends of Euripides, fellow exiles from Athens. Among them were Agathon the tragedian, Timotheus the musician, Zeuxis the painter, and very probably the historian Thucydides. *The Bacchae,* Euripides' last and most beautifully turned tragedy, was written at the court of Archelaus. Paradoxical to the last,

A scene painted inside a sixth-century-B.C. cup shows the king of Cyrene in Libya supervising the weighing of silphium, a medicinal plant, for export.

he made it an anti-intellectual plea. King Pentheus, the play's hero and victim, refuses on moral and intellectual grounds to credit the demonic powers of the wine god Dionysus. Thereupon his own mother, being possessed by the god, tears him to pieces and carries off his head. That is the sort of thing which can happen, Euripides says in effect, to stiff-necked skeptics. But far more typical of his message in general is this mordant passage from Bellerophon (translated by the British poet John Addington Symonds):

> *Doth some one say that there be gods above?*
> *There are not; no, there are not. Let no fool,*
> *Led by the old false fable, thus deceive you.*
> *Look at the facts themselves, yielding my words*
> *No undue credence: for I say that kings*
> *Kill, rob, break oaths, lay cities waste by fraud,*
> *And doing thus are happier than those*
> *Who live calm pious lives day after day.*
> *How many little States that serve the gods*
> *Are subject to the godless but more strong,*
> *Made slaves by might of a superior army!*
> *And you, if any ceased from work and prayed*
> *To gods, nor gathered in his livelihood,*
> *Would learn gods are not. All Divinity*
> *Is built up from our good and evil luck.*

Attic theater had its roots in ancient rites. Tragedy evolved from sacrificial ceremony—perhaps involving humans, but no one knows for certain. At some point, goats came to be offered up on the altar of Dionysus, and the word "tragedy" itself comes from the Greek for "goat-cry." So all three of the great Athenian tragedians worked within limits set by the concept of sacrifice to an implacable deity. Their protagonists might take philosophical or even antitheistic positions, and yet, ready or not, they usually had to die. Comedy, which was also very much a part of Athens' dramatic festivals, sprang from rustic fertility rites. These, in their earliest form, may well have included ritual copulation. Phallic romps and processions followed. Masked "satyrs," who were both sexual nature-spirits and figures of fun, were introduced. These too found a voice: not a goat-cry but rough and heady mockery.

So writers of Attic comedy also had a tradition to obey. They were compelled to be wild, biting, and obscene. Among the first masters of this difficult art were Cratinus and Eupolis, whose works are lost to us except for a few fragments. We have a crackling little attack on Admiral Cimon from Eupolis' pen. Cratinus roasted Pericles as "our own squill-headed Zeus" and "the dear son of Double-Dealing and Long-Time." But the only writer of old Attic comedy whose works we still possess in any quantity was Aristophanes.

Born just in the middle of the fifth century B.C., Aristophanes lived to lighten Athens' heart now and again throughout the darkest period of the Peloponnesian War. Like many humorists, Aristophanes was a conservative at heart, and this instinct found constant reinforcement in the fact that while he lived the times got worse and worse. He brilliantly inveighed against the war which was ruining Athens. He dared put the demagogue Cleon, the man who inherited much of Pericles' power, on stage and pillory him as a vicious character. One of his plays, now lost, included a satyr chorus of Athens' so-called allies singing in their chains on a treadmill. That production, it seems, got Aristophanes into serious trouble. He later complained of having received a near-fatal rolling in the dirt, and perhaps he was put on trial for treason. But Athens had real need of Aristophanes. The people loved him so that they even permitted him to slug the great loud-growling Cleon "in the belly," as he himself put it.

Heavenly tyrants received comparable treatment from Aristophanes. His most marvelous surviving work, *The Birds,* is a sort of dream in which sharp-beaked and eloquent songsters like himself successfully revolt against the Olympian pantheon. In that comedy appears Prometheus, the ancient Titan and friend to man. Half a century before, Aeschylus had shown that same Prometheus crucified upon a Caucasian peak by Zeus. Aristophanes had the audacious profanity to present the Titan holding a large umbrella as protection from "Them Above."

In another wonderful play, *The Clouds,* Aristophanes poked fun at the imperturbable Socrates. It is said that when *The Clouds* was first performed, Socrates happened to be in the audience. Obligingly, the homely philosopher got up from his seat to let the audience compare his true face with the comic mask of the actor on stage. At one point in the play, the sage reveals to an inquirer that clouds make rain. "A

pretty proof," says the inquirer, "and to think I used to believe the rain was just Zeus pissing through a sieve."

The men of Athens, Aristophanes understood, were bringing their own city to destruction. In fact the war with Sparta reduced a world to dust. Men, who were raised in the ancient Homeric tradition that to kill is excellent, could find no way to make peace. Would women do any better? That startling possibility was the germ of Aristophanes' most overtly political play: *Lysistrata.* The comedy embodies the earliest women's liberation movement on record. Lysistrata, the heroine, persuades the women of Athens to go on strike against the Peloponnesian War. They will not sleep with their husbands, they swear, until it is all over. But, an Athenian magistrate objects, it's not so easy to achieve a peace treaty. "How can we do it?" There would be no problem, Lysistrata replies, if only one were to deal with "this weary Hellenic entanglement" in the same way that women handle a fleece. And she goes on:

> *First, in the washing-tub*
> *plunge it, and scour it, and cleanse it from grease,*
> *Purging away all the filth and the nastiness;*
> *then on the table expand it and lay,*
> *Beating out all that is worthless and mischievous,*
> *picking burrs and the thistles away.*
> *Next, for the clubs, the cabals, and the coteries,*
> *banding unrighteously, office to win,*
> *Treat them to clots in the wool, and dissever them,*
> *lopping the heads that are forming therein.*
> *Then you should card it, and comb it, and mingle it,*
> *all in one Basket of love and of unity,*
> *Citizens, visitors, strangers, and sojourners,*
> *all the entire, undivided community.*
> *Know you a fellow in debt to the Treasury?*
> *Mingle him merrily in with the rest.*
> *Also remember the cities, our colonies,*
> *outlying states in the east and the west,*
> *Scattered about to a distance surrounding us,*
> *these are our shreds and our fragments of wool;*

Greek fantasy produced such wild creatures as the satyr, holding a vase at left, and the Boreades, pursuing Harpies and a sphinx on the plate, above.

> *These to one mighty political aggregate*
> *tenderly, carefully, gather and pull,*
> *Twining them all in one thread of good fellowship;*
> *thence a magnificent bobbin to spin,*
> *Weaving a garment of comfort and dignity,*
> *worthily wrapping the People therein.*

With Aspasia's help, the irreplaceable Pericles had handled Athens' problems of empire in more or less that way. But by the time Aristophanes wrote *Lysistrata,* Pericles was long dead and Athenian culture had already become a partial ruin. What had gone wrong with Periclean policy? Was it inevitable? The first historian to sense the crucial significance of these questions was Thucydides, who began his career in the Periclean circle and lived through the entire Peloponnesian War. Serving very briefly as a general, he was sent to relieve a northern city which was under Spartan attack. Thucydides arrived too late and accomplished nothing. The Athenian Assembly punished him with a twenty-year sentence of exile. Frustrated as a man of action, he turned thoughtful indeed. He began his history of the Peloponnesian War, he writes, "in the belief that it was going to be a great war and more worth writing about than any of those which had taken place in the past. . . . This was the greatest disturbance in the history of the Hellenes, affecting also a large part of the non-Hellenic world and indeed I might almost say the whole of mankind." As the struggle continued on and on, Thucydides came to understand with iron clarity that it was not so much the "greatness" of the thing as the terrible lessons it involved which would command the attention of posterity. "It may well be," he decided, "that my history will seem less easy to read because of the absence in it of a romantic element. It will be enough for me, however, if these words of mine are judged useful by those who want to understand clearly events which happened in the past and which (human nature being what it is) will, at some time or other and in much the same ways, be repeated in the future. My work is not a piece of writing designed to meet the taste of an immediate public, but was done to last for ever."

He meant, of course, to denigrate Herodotus, his only major predecessor. Thucydides had no way of knowing that there was room for

both writers on the shelf of immortal historians. Those with a taste for stark facts, strongly moral positions, and inexorable logic, naturally prefer Thucydides' account of his war to the one which Herodotus had given of the struggle against Persia. But on the other hand, people who lean to richness of detail, encyclopedic thought, and compassionate characterization will always put Herodotus first. In terms of our contemporary disciplines, Thucydides especially appeals to social scientists, and Herodotus to anthropologists. The books of both men set precedents which are by no means exhausted even today. Among the specific weaknesses for which Thucydides appears to fault Herodotus, were the older man's apparent haziness in matters of battle and his evocation of Themistocles as all too human. Thucydides himself shines, not surprisingly, in describing military tactics. He judges people rather strictly by their public accomplishments, and to him Themistocles was a man who "beyond all others deserves our admiration." In a typically sweeping and forceful passage, Thucydides enumerates the inherent abilities of the trickster who saved the West, and concludes: "He was particularly remarkable at looking into the future and seeing there the hidden possibilities for good or evil. To sum him up in a few words, it may be said that through force of genius and by rapidity of action this man was supreme at doing precisely the right thing at precisely the right moment."

Herodotus might have allowed himself a rueful smile at the one-sidedness of that. However, few could deny that Themistocles was one of the three greatest leaders in Greek history. The other two were Pericles and, of course, Alexander the Great. Each of the three unfolded a new destiny for Greece. Themistocles nurtured the bud of Greek liberty; Pericles brought Greek culture to blossom; and Alexander sowed her seeds from Egypt all the way to Afghanistan. But are such men fathers of destiny or are they its children?

Take Pericles, for instance, and his inalienably paradoxical legacy. By doing everything he could to promote and strengthen Athens' maritime empire, Pericles was not serving Athenian interests alone. On the contrary, he was trying to overcome the already obsolete fragmentation of Greece into warring city-states. He had the imagination to call an inter-city conference for just this purpose. His idea seems to have been the setting up of a federation directed against possible Persian domina-

tion—much the same thing that the philosopher Thales had long before proposed for Ionia. There is some analogy here to Europe's Common Market, and even to the United Nations organization. We in the twentieth century are struggling to free ourselves from obsolete aspects of nationalism, just as the Greeks wrestled with obsolete city-statism twenty-five centuries ago. We run risks very similar in kind, though not in scope, to those which brought Athens low. For one thing, our world seems split down the middle on ideological grounds just as was Greece. The inter-city conference which Pericles proposed never came off, because Sparta and her allies considered it a trick to promote the Athenian way of life and politics. Perhaps there was that in it, too. Although practically a dictator by force of personality, Pericles did firmly believe in democracy, commercial expansion, and capitalism. The Spartan position was the opposite: favoring government by committee, a conservative land-based economy, and communism of a kind whereby the state rather than private interest decided matters. Such diametrically opposed political and economic views were bound to create friction between Sparta and Athens. And this in turn might well bring on a war, as Pericles apparently foresaw. Instead of awaiting the worst, in any case, he went out to meet it. His way of doing so was to form alliances with formerly neutral and potentially powerful Greek city-states such as the western island of Corfu. When that failed to rouse the Spartans, Pericles came down hard on other city-states within the Spartan orbit of influence, forcing them to beg assistance from Sparta. This resulted in a war atmosphere with feverish negotiations throughout the whole mosaic of Greek city-states. In general, the Peloponnesus including Corinth, and central Greece including Thebes, sided with Sparta. By and large, the Greek islands and Ionia remained on Athens' side, but many of these were forced to do so. Throughout the Greek world a new generation of men were growing up without experience of war. Their fathers described the Greek repulse of Persia as a glorious thing—which it had truly been. The young men were ready to seek glory in their turn. They had no idea what that might mean. But Sparta, as the only state with a standing army and a ruling officer class, did maintain a relatively realistic attitude. The Spartans sent a final ultimatum to Athens: "Sparta wants peace. Peace is still possible if you will give the Hellenes their freedom."

Ruins at Delphi, the oracular shrine to Apollo on Mount Parnassus

At that point of decision, Pericles made a crucial address to the Athenian Assembly. He was already sixty-four years of age, and possibly he wished to bring the war on soon in order to command it while he still could. Be that as it may, he urged his fellow citizens to give the Spartans a harsh answer. Any concessions, he told them in effect, would only encourage subversion within Athens' empire. The tribute which Athens had received and was receiving from her subject states made her very much richer than the Peloponnesian alliance. Her enemies would soon find out, Pericles added, that war is expensive. Granting the fact that the Peloponnesian land forces were superior, Athens held undisputed command at sea. Therefore, Pericles advised, the Athenians should make an island of their city walls and not offer battle on land. The walls of Athens, by the way, had been included in Pericles' great building program, and they were spectacularly strong. Under Pericles' direction the entire port of Athens, the Piraeus, had been enclosed and joined to the city by parallel bastions several miles long. Undoubtedly, Pericles warned, the Peloponnesians would invade Attica and lay waste the Athenians' country villages, farms, and estates. "And if I thought I could persuade you to do it," he told them, "I would urge you to go out and lay waste your property with your own hands and show the Peloponnesians that it is not for the sake of this that you are likely to give in to them." By keeping strictly defensive in posture at home while ravaging the Peloponnesian seacoast on naval expeditions, Athens could soon fight Sparta to a standstill. That was Pericles' conclusion, but he added one final and fateful "if." Things are going to be all right, he said, "if only you will make up your minds not to add to the empire while the war is in progress, and not to go out of your way to involve yourselves in new perils. What I fear is not the enemy's strategy but our own mistakes."

Was the war which then ensued really inevitable? Thucydides, for one, believed it was. But the reason he gives is not ideological. "What made war inevitable," Thucydides asserts simply, "was the growth of Athenian power and the fear which this caused Sparta."

For the first year or so the struggle went precisely as Pericles had planned. Greece is about the size of Portugal and yet possesses a coastline as long as Spain's. This geographical peculiarity, which reflects the vast number of the Greek islands and the multiplicate convolutions of

Greek shores, was what put Athenian sea power on equal terms with Spartan land power. It made conflict between the two fretful and indecisive. Imagine a grisly bear and a great white shark which are determined to destroy each other and cannot find the means to do so. Soothsayers in Athens and elsewhere were soon repeating a prophecy to the effect that the war would last "thrice nine years"—although some were stoned to death for such seeming defeatism.

Sparta had received a kind of go-ahead from Delphi. "I shall be fighting on your side," Apollo had assured the Spartans through the lips of the oracle, "whether you invoke me or not." For the present, there was much burning of farmhouses and chopping down of vineyards and olive trees, but little actual bloodshed. When the Peloponnesian army appeared, the people of Attica all crowded within Athens' walls. When Athenian sea raiders struck at Sparta's allies, they too retreated for the moment to their own fortified cities. Skirmishes were fought, but no major battles.

At the end of the first year of war, a funeral ceremony was held in honor of the few Athenian dead. Pericles took this opportunity to make an address concerning the way of life which Athens meant to defend. Thucydides makes no claim to repeat Pericles' words verbatim. They give every indication of having been polished by the historian's pen. But, nonetheless, the speech deserves quotation in part. It says a lot about what did make Athens great. Here are some key points, then,

Circular ballots, like these, were cast by jurors in Greek law courts to determine a defendant's guilt or innocence.

from Pericles' most famous oration as recorded in Thucydides' history:

"Our constitution is called a democracy because power is in the hands not of a minority but of the whole people. When it is a question of settling private disputes, everyone is equal before the law; when it is a question of putting one person before another in positions of public responsibility, what counts is not membership of a particular class, but the actual ability which the man possesses. No one, so long as he has it in him to be of service to the state, is kept in political obscurity because of poverty. And, just as our political life is free and open, so is our day-to-day life in our relations with each other. We do not get into a state with our next-door neighbor if he enjoys himself in his own way, nor do we give him the kind of black looks which, though they do no real harm, still do hurt people's feelings. We are free and tolerant in our private lives; but in public affairs we keep to the law. This is because it commands our deep respect. . . .

"When our work is over, we are in a position to enjoy all kinds of recreation for our spirits. There are various kinds of contests and sacrifices regularly throughout the year; in our own homes we find a beauty and a good taste which delight us every day and which drive away our cares. Then the greatness of our city brings it about that all the good things from all over the world flow in to us, so that to us it seems just as natural to enjoy foreign goods as our own local products. . . .

"Our love of what is beautiful does not lead to extravagance; our love of things of the mind does not make us soft. . . . We are capable at the same time of taking risks and of estimating them beforehand. Others are brave out of ignorance; and, when they stop to think, they begin to fear. But the man who can most truly be accounted brave is he who best knows the meaning of what is sweet in life and of what is terrible, and then goes out undeterred to meet what is to come."

In all that, there was no boasting. Pericles told the truth, and what he had to say still stands as a political ideal for many of us today. In point of fact, these often-quoted passages did not fail to influence the creators of the American Constitution. Pericles speaks with quiet dignity across the centuries.

According to Homer, Apollo had taken the Trojan side when Troy was being besieged by the Achaeans. The god shot arrows of plague into the Achaean camp, bringing death first to the animals there and

afterward to thousands of warriors. Now, as the Peloponnesian War stumbled on through a second, third, and fourth year of attrition, Apollo shot arrows of plague into crowded Athens. The disease had apparently broken out in Egypt, and ravaged parts of the Persian Empire. Rats riding in grain ships probably brought it to the Piraeus. From there it spread throughout the city slowly, flickering out and flaring up again from month to month and year to year until perhaps a quarter of the population was destroyed. Pericles himself died of the plague. Thucydides was one of the few to contract the disease and somehow survive. His dispassionate description of it makes sickening reading even yet. Keeping in mind our capabilities for waging germ warfare, one shudders to recall Thucydides' warning that history repeats itself.

Seeing Athens weakened by plague and four years of conflict, the island-city of Mytilene attempted to revolt. But Athens still possessed sufficient power to crush uprisings anywhere within reach of her ships. Mytilene surrendered and accepted an Athenian garrison. Meanwhile, the ringleaders of the revolt were transported to Athens for trial. In the Assembly, a tanner's son from the Piraeus made an inflammatory speech suggesting that the entire male population of Mytilene should be killed and the women and children sold into slavery. The speaker's name was Cleon. He stood for the Athenian poor and for social welfare at home coupled with the utmost brutality in prosecuting war. Now that Pericles was dead, Cleon's coarse and colorful self-assurance made him the mightiest politician in Athens. His motion for a massacre at Mytilene was passed by the Assembly, and a trireme was dispatched that same day to see that the Assembly's instructions were carried out.

Next morning, however, many Athenians had second thoughts on the subject of Mytilene. The Assembly reconvened. One of Cleon's opponents rose to suggest a more lenient course. He made no effort at all to plead the islanders' case, nor did he appeal to the Athenians' own better nature. The war had already gone on too long for that. The minds and hearts of most Athenian citizens were already closed to such considerations of mercy. The immortal brilliance of Athenian achievement in particular during the fifth century B.C. cannot excuse, although it does serve to obscure, the bloodthirstiness of the ancient Greeks. Compassion never entered into the Athenian debate on Mytilene. Expediency, however, did. It was argued that future revolts would be

rendered all the more desperate if the revolutionaries were given no options except to succeed or die in the attempt. The point seemed well taken. The Assembly reversed itself. A second trireme was sent out to overtake the first, and countermand the previous orders. The first ship had a twenty-four-hour start. It arrived at Mytilene alone. And then, just as the commander of the Athenian garrison was unrolling the scroll upon which the sentence of massacre was written, the second ship sailed in. "So narrow," Thucydides concludes, "had been the escape of Mytilene." But the thousand or more islanders previously transported to Athens were, he adds, executed. Moreover, as the war progressed, atrocities worse than the proposed massacre at Mytilene were in fact carried out elsewhere.

Class differences much exacerbated the Peloponnesian War. Sparta supported revolutionary cliques of "the best people," that is to say landed aristocrats, in the cities under Athenian leadership. Athens meanwhile gave aid and comfort to dispossessed "democratic insurrectionists" within the Peloponnesian alliance. Thus, as Thucydides relates, "revolutions broke out in city after city, and in places where the revolutions occurred late the knowledge of what had happened previously in other places caused still new extravagances in the methods of seizing power and by unheard-of atrocities in revenge. To fit in with the change of events, words, too, had to change their usual meanings. What used to be described as a thoughtless act of aggression was now regarded as the courage one would expect to find in a party member; to think of the future and wait was merely another way of saying one was a coward; any idea of moderation was just an attempt to disguise one's unmanly character; ability to understand a question from all sides meant that one was totally unfitted for action. Fanatical enthusiasm was the mark of a real man, and to plot against an enemy behind his back was perfectly legitimate self-defense. Anyone who held violent opinions could always be trusted, and anyone who objected to them became a suspect. . . . As the result of these revolutions, there was a general deterioration of character throughout the Greek world. The simple way of looking at things, which is so much the mark of a noble nature, was regarded as a ridiculous quality and soon ceased to exist."

Strictly military tactics were changing also. The heavily armed hoplite or citizen foot soldier had won the day at Marathon and again at

An ornamented bronze mirror with a stand in the form of a female figure, made in the second half of the fifth century B.C.

Plataea. But this new war set Greek against Greek and not against a foreign power, so the fighting abilities of the hoplites more or less canceled each other out. Experimentation with new techniques for killing soldiers and leveling cities became the rule. Ingenious catapults and counterfortifications were devised for siege purposes. Cavalry was increasingly employed for hit-and-run attacks and cleanup sweeps. Light-armed mercenaries, slingers, and javelin throwers from the semi-barbarous north were brought in to harass regular infantry. Orthodox generals were upstaged by amateurs with fresh ideas. The demagogue Cleon, for one, masterminded an attack on an islet off Pylos which netted 292 hoplite prisoners of whom no less than 120 were Spartan officers. Cleon made sure that the enemy was worn out with thirst and decimated by constantly repeated archery attacks before coming to grips. He brought his prisoners back in triumph to Athens, where the people regarded them incredulously. These hulking fellows in chains, with their rough woolen cloaks and long shaggy hair, appeared like beasts of prey in a zoo. Mockingly, an Athenian asked one prisoner whether perhaps the only brave Spartans were those who had been killed in battle. The Spartan glowered, thought a bit, and then replied pithily as was Laconian custom: "Arrows would be worth a great deal if they could pick out brave men from cowards." In fact the new preponderance of missiles and mobility in battlecraft had put Spartan military principles—never surrender, never retreat—out of date.

Cleon's death came as a boon to Athens. The city's worst warmonger fell at last in an insignificant battle at Amphipolis, far to the north on the Thracian coast. Sparta's best general, Brasidas, died in the same battle. By then the war had lasted a decade. The sufferings of Greece throughout that time had been severe, but they had not substantially altered the political picture. Perhaps the scales of power had tilted a few degrees in Athens' direction; nothing more. But with Cleon out of the way, the war party no longer dominated the Athenian Assembly. A rich, conservative, and successful old general named Nicias now assured the citizens that their strivings had, after all, made the world safe for Athenian empire; and, naturally, democracy. Both sides had good reasons for making peace. Sparta would probably sign almost any treaty for the sake of her hoplites from Pylos, whom Athens still held. Nicias had been friendly to those prisoners, and eased their sufferings

Chariot horses painted on a black-figured amphora of about 525 B.C.

in every way possible. Being a military man, he understood the chanciness of war. So Nicias urged the Assembly to ratify an armistice, at least. He had his way. A treaty was drawn up, which neither side was to honor, and some years of uneasy truce followed. This was the cold war known to contemporary observers as the Peace of Nicias.

Peace fell victim to the machinations of one of the most remarkable persons in all Greek history, Alcibiades, who managed to embrace all sides of the conflict. No one can say whether in the long run he helped or harmed any particular cause. Yet at the time he seemed a young whirlwind, an eloquent stirrer-up of men from the speaker's platform, and in war an irresistible strategist. This singularly subversive person must have seemed especially baffling to the clear mind of Thucydides. Alcibiades passed like a speeding atomic particle through ideological and cultural barriers. Writers, being wedded to words and ideas, are not very apt to give such a man as Alcibiades his due. But the urbane Plutarch, whose richly anecdotal *Lives* stands next to Herodotus and Thucydides as a source book of ancient Greek history, achieves the most convincing portrait.

"Even the chameleon cannot take on the color of white," Plutarch remarks, "but Alcibiades was able to associate with good and bad alike, and never found a characteristic which he could not imitate or practice. Thus, in Sparta, he was all for physical exercise, the simple life, and an appearance of forbidding austerity; in Ionia for luxury, pleasure, and indolence; in Thrace he could drink with the best; in Thessaly he was never out of the saddle, and when he found himself in the company of Tissaphernes the satrap, he surpassed even the magnificence of the Persian in his pomp and extravagance. It was not so much that he could pass with ease from one type of behavior to another, nor that his own character was transformed in every case; but when he saw that by following his own inclinations he would give offense to his associates, he promptly assumed whatever manner or exterior was appropriate to the situation."

The final installment of the Peloponnesian War was even longer and more dreadful than the first part had been. It abounded in confusion, and yet from the very distant perspective of the present time it all seems bound up with the flashing, many-sided life of Alcibiades. He came from an exceedingly rich and distinguished family. When his

father was killed in battle, Pericles became his foster father. Alcibiades grew up under the tutelage of Pericles and Aspasia, and in adolescence passed from their hands to those of Socrates. He had his first taste of battle at the philosopher's side, on a campaign in Boeotia. When Alcibiades fell wounded, Socrates stood over him and saved his life. When he came into possession of his fortune, Alcibiades determined to spend it magnificently. He entered seven chariots in the games at Olympia, and saw them take first, third, and fourth place. This triumph might strike some thoughtful people today as frivolous, but it did not seem that way to the vast majority of Alcibiades' contemporaries. They set sport next to war in importance. So Alcibiades became the acknowledged leader of the younger generation at Athens. He was the man most likely to get Athens moving again. For wealth and style, Alcibiades might be compared to the Kennedy family all rolled into one.

Sparta herself seemed no more than a stumbling block to a person of such fiery imaginative force as Alcibiades. He managed to persuade the Athenian Assembly to attempt the conquest of a second Peloponnesus in the west, namely, Sicily. The fact that Sicily's leading city, Syracuse, was almost as eminent as Athens bothered him not the slightest. Nicias, naturally, warned against sending an armada to subdue Sicily, but the Assembly laughed off the old general's fears. They set Nicias together with Alcibiades and Lamachus in charge of the expedition. Filled with rejoicing, and in high hopes of achieving imperishable glory, the Athenian armada sailed. It reached Sicily safely, and the cautious generalship of Nicias kept it out of trouble for some time thereafter. But Alcibiades meanwhile found himself recalled to Athens on a charge for which death was the penalty. He was accused of having profaned the mysteries of Eleusis by performing a sort of Black Mass with himself as the high priest. His political opponents may well have fabricated this charge, but on the other hand it fits Alcibiades' character.

Rather than face trial, in any case, Alcibiades slipped away to Sparta. There he charmed old enemies so much that they let him take charge of Spartan strategy against Athens. Alcibiades counseled them first to send aid and officers to Syracuse. This would bring about the absolute defeat and ruin of the expedition commanded by Nicias. Then, Alcibiades suggested that Sparta fortify a position within striking distance of Athens, and place a permanent garrison there as a thorn in the city's

side. While Sparta's King Agis was away on that business, Alcibiades seduced his wife. Typically, the young turncoat asserted that he took the queen to bed not for pleasure but to assure that his descendants would one day rule over Sparta. His next stroke of policy was to implement a Spartan alliance with Persia. Alcibiades sailed out to the east to take up residence at the court of a Persian satrap as Sparta's ambassador. According to some historians, his ostensible purpose was to draw the Persian navy into the war on the side of Sparta, and crush Athens forever. But he had earned the well-deserved enmity of King Agis, and so he had thought it best to switch his allegiance once again. Alcibiades' secret advice to the Persians was that they should remain on the sidelines and watch the Greeks go on destroying each other. By now, the situation at Athens was growing desperate. It became apparent that Athens' one remaining hope lay with her prodigal son: Alcibiades. If he were to swing the Persian fleet into action on the Athenian side, things might yet be saved. So motions were made and carried by the Assembly to exonerate Alcibiades and beg him to come home again.

Alcibiades accepted the invitation. But first he set out to prove that Athens could still work wonders even without Persian assistance. Taking command of the much-restricted Athenian forces in Ionia, he mounted a lightning campaign of conquest and retribution which put Sparta on the defensive in that area. Then and only then did he sail home. His ships were garlanded with enemy shields from stem to stern. The figureheads of no less than two hundred triremes captured or shattered by Alcibiades lay aboard. According to some legends, Alcibiades' flagship put into the Piraeus with a purple sail hoisted, as if he were leading a band of revelers home from a drinking party. He had come full circle and his success, that is to say his personal success, was complete. But the war with Sparta dragged on. A naval battle at which Alcibiades was not present went against Athens. The fickle Assembly thereupon removed Alcibiades from command. He "retired" at age forty-six to a castle in Phrygia and a love affair with a famous courtesan named Timandra. There he was surrounded one night and assassinated by unknown enemies.

Meanwhile a pickup navy of mercenaries financed by Persia and commanded by a Spartan named Lysander engaged the bulk of Athens' remaining ships in battle for the Hellespont. That waterway to the

Terra-cotta statuettes, from top (clockwise): a cooking lesson, a man cooking, a bather, a barber and client, and a housewife peering into her oven.

Black Sea and the grain markets of Scythia was the weakest link in Athenian power. Simply by blocking it, Lysander knew, he could starve Athens. In the event, by superior strategy, he destroyed about 160 Athenian triremes. He took more than 3,000 prisoners, and executed every one. That blow meant the end of the war.

Famine forced final surrender upon Athens in the year 404 B.C. There is a story that Lysander sent a triumphant dispatch home to Sparta consisting of only three words: "Athens is taken." The Spartan authorities are said to have returned this message: " 'Taken' would have been enough."

The terms, predictably, were tough. Lysander called upon Athens to give up all but a dozen triremes, and to dismantle the fortifications of the Piraeus and the long walls connecting them to the upper city. The choice lay, he told the Athenian Assembly, between accepting those conditions and being slaughtered. "After the Athenians had finally given way to all Lysander's demands," Plutarch concludes, "he sent for a great company of flute girls from the city and collected all those who were in his camp. Then to the sound of their music, he pulled down the walls and burned the ships, while the allies garlanded themselves with flowers, rejoiced together, and hailed that day as the beginning of freedom for Greece."

Pericles had promised, a generation before, to make Athens "the education of Hellas." That promise was fulfilled, but not in a manner expected by him. He had regarded Athens as a goddess of arts and ideas, and mistress of the seas, not as a potential sacrifice. The education which Athens provided was partly a bitter one, for her own people. But that education goes on working and spreading endlessly, like ripples from a stone thrown in a pond. Phidias, Aeschylus, Sophocles, Euripides, and Aristophanes were all Athenians. Art and literature are very slow, as a rule, to influence public affairs. A masterpiece makes itself felt, not merely over years but across centuries. Yet curious exceptions to this pattern may occur, and here is one of them. At the end of the Athenian debacle in Sicily, Syracuse held some seven thousand prisoners. They were penned for months in a deep quarry, where the vast majority perished. But, as Plutarch records, "a few were rescued because of their knowledge of Euripides, for it seems that the Sicilians were more devoted to his poetry than any other Greeks living outside

the mother country. Even the smallest fragments of his verses were gleaned from every stranger who set foot on their island, and they took delight in exchanging these quotations with one another. At any rate, there is a tradition that many of the Athenian soldiers who returned home safely visited Euripides to thank him for their deliverance which they owed to his poetry." That story speaks volumes, in its way. Apparently, "the education of Hellas" never ceased, not even during the moments of Greece's worst agony.

The whole Peloponnesian War, counting in the troubled peace of Nicias, lasted twenty-seven years almost to the day. You will recall the soothsayer's prediction that it was fated to persist for "thrice-nine years." Thucydides, unlike Herodotus, did not believe in oracles; yet he conscientiously recorded this instance of their accuracy.

Wars, like chapters, come to an end at last. But history never stops. And even in peacetime, as will be seen in the chapter to come, the turns which history takes may prove astonishing.

CHAPTER V

THE
INFINITE
AFTERGLOW

T he arts do not progress. They bud, blossom, and pass away to seed again, along with the cultures which made them possible. The gradual expansion of human consciousness takes place in a more continuous way. The poems, plays, sculptures, and shrines created by the ancient Greeks are incomparable, of course. But the concomitant onrush of Greek science and philosophy was, quite simply, unique. The great questions which man puts to himself are unforgettable—once they have been proposed—and the putting of just such questions was to an extraordinary degree the privilege of the ancient Greeks. The most persistent questioner of them all, Socrates, set problems which no thinking person can afford to ignore, even today.

Socrates had few solutions to suggest. He preached "the good life," mainly by example. But his own life was a model which no ordinary person could imitate. He was not in favor of instruction, but of mutual inquiry in conversation; he practiced dialectics unceasingly with everyone he met but wrote nothing at all. Thoughts on paper, he explained, would have no means of defending themselves. Concepts were living forces, and he a soldier in their wars. Indeed, battle was in Socrates'

*The time-weary face of a philosopher, from a third-century-*B.C. *bronze*

blood. He took part as a hoplite in two hard-fought campaigns, and earned distinction each time. Alcibiades, for one, praised his coolness in action. But this virtue of Socrates' was most strongly revealed many years later when he made his final and complete gift to mankind: his martyrdom.

Before considering that event, let us look back for a moment or two at the thinkers who came just before Socrates. The eldest of these was Heraclitus of Ephesus, who found some glimmering of truth in a hearth fire. Nature is process, Heraclitus proclaimed. The world burns, as it were, with life. "As gold is exchanged for goods," he wrote, "and goods for gold; so fire feeds all things, and all things feed the fire." Needless to say, the actual relation of the sun to life on earth seems very close to Heraclitus' description. He said also: "Everything flows: you cannot step into the same river twice." This again appears a strangely prophetic intuition. Electronic microscopes and the like enable us to see something of what Heraclitus guessed must be true, namely, the endless swirling and flowing of atomic existence.

Parmenides of Elea, in Italy, did not place the same trust in Nature. Disregard it, he said in effect. Everything gives the appearance of coming into being and passing away again, but that is illusion. What is, is; and what is not, is not. So, no actual change ever happens. Change would involve some interaction between being and not-being. This is impossible, since not-being cannot interact with anything. The world might be likened metaphorically to an elephant which five blind men— the five senses—examine part by part and fail to comprehend. Only when one goes beyond empirical methods is the world seen as it truly is—a solid, unmoving, and immutable sphere. God and the world are one and eternal. Human experience, Parmenides concluded, is just the shadow of a dream which has nothing to do with how things really are.

Empedocles of Acragas, in Sicily, argued against Parmenides. One ought to credit each of the five senses, he said, in the way in which that particular sense is clear. Earth, air, fire, and water are the four immutable elements which make up the world. Admitting that there can be no interaction between being and not-being, there is a constant play of association and dissociation among the four elements which produce the changing phenomena of the world we observe. Love and discord rule the endless interrelations between them.

Democritus of Abdera, in Thrace, had a different notion. Instead of fretting over absolutely abstract concepts such as being and not-being, he suggested, why not translate those terms into things? Namely, "atoms, and the void." The word "atoms" is Greek and means "uncuttables." Democritus had in mind something a good deal smaller and more autonomous than our smashable kind. They were spherical, immutable, and eternal. Given "the void" in which to move, atoms could build up like a coral reef to create everything in the world, and just as readily fall away again. This picture transposes the not-being posited by Parmenides into real existence: space. It allows for the return of motion, of eternal flux, as envisioned by Heraclitus.

But what is it that conjures up all creation from those autonomous atoms? Anaxagoras of Clazomenae, Pericles' mentor, proposed a tentative answer. First, he said, atoms are no mere building blocks or dead units of living structures. They act more like seedlings from which great things unfold. Amongst these innumerable seedlings, Anaxagoras instructed, are some finer than all the rest, which had best be described as mind stuff. Mind works through every part of the mixture in a fermenting, organizing, and fructifying manner. This idea thrilled Socrates in particular. The younger man was eager to believe Anaxagoras, as he later confessed. But, sadly enough, Anaxagoras could produce no proofs. His argument remained pure speculation. Its best claim to authenticity was that the concept seemed consistent with itself and aesthetically pleasing.

That kind of claim never satisfied Socrates for long. He was extremely open to ideas—no man more so—but ruthless in his destruction of them. One anecdote tells of his borrowing a treatise by Heraclitus and afterward returning it with a typically double-edged comment. "This is truly profound," Socrates said, adding, "You'd have to be a sponge-diver to get to the bottom of it." His own approach to things could be summed up in a dry epigram by the poet Epicharmus of Syracuse:

A sober sense of honest doubt
Keeps human reason hale and stout.

The best support which Socrates found for this viewpoint came from the medical profession. Hippocrates of Cos, who may fairly be

called the father of modern medicine, insisted upon close observation as the key to all diagnosis. Socrates, who was his contemporary, did much the same. But what Socrates chose to diagnose concerned the mind rather than the body.

Visiting professors of ethics, persuasion, and politics added much to Athens' intellectual luster in Socrates' time. Sophists, they called themselves. Their leader, Protagoras, proclaimed: "Man is the measure of all things." Human institutions are not sacred in themselves. They should be changed as occasion demands. Such was the main thrust of Protagoras' teaching. It impressed Pericles, for one, so much that he employed Protagoras to draw up the legislation for a new Athenian colony in Italy.

The scepticism of the Sophists found a sympathetic echo in Socrates, but he felt that they should not accept payment for lecturing and that they should seek higher ends than rhetoric for its own sake. One of their number, Gorgias, argued this way: "There is no truth. If truth existed it could not be known. If it were known, it could not be communicated." That does indeed seem to put teaching itself out of court.

Socrates' own position was: "Only God is wise." The Delphic oracle had declared that there was no man wiser than Socrates.

The philosopher, who had respect for the oracle, was deeply troubled by this pronouncement. After some thought, he concluded that the oracle really meant that "there is no man wiser than Socrates, because he alone understands that he knows nothing." Socrates did not mean that there is nothing to be known. Unlike Gorgias, he believed in the existence of eternal truths to which men are blind; unlike Protagoras, he held a very unflattering opinion of the powers of the human mind in uncovering such truth.

These subtle and yet fundamental differences between Socrates' viewpoint and that of the Sophists were lost on most Athenians. Socrates' contemporaries tended to see him as a scornful and cynical companion to dangerous young men. Alcibiades, after all, had been one of his closest friends, as were leading members of the puppet government which Sparta imposed upon beaten Athens. The "Thirty Tyrants," as they were called, executed hundreds of Athenian citizens for having "democratic sympathies." Socrates spoke out boldly against this policy, yet he went unpunished. This made him all the more suspect.

A Hellenistic statuette reveals a homely, snub-nosed Socrates, who nevertheless possesses a certain air of dignity.

In the year 403 B.C., street riots overthrew the puppet government. Democracy was restored. Sparta made no move to prevent this, because she found herself embroiled in new troubles with other city-states. Athens, therefore, was able to begin her long but relatively peaceful climb back to commercial and cultural supremacy in Greece. Meanwhile, the Athenians looked around, as people always will, for some scapegoat on whom to blame their recent troubles. Their eyes fixed upon the aged Socrates, who still surrounded himself with bright young friends, and still raised embarrassing questions. So he was brought to trial on two charges: first, "Socrates disbelieves in the gods"; and secondly, "He corrupts the young." The penalty demanded was death.

Socrates chose to defend himself, typically enough, by an ironical and steadfast sort of indirection. He made no excuses at all. Instead, he demonstrated that his accusers were fools and that the city as a whole could use a strong dose of humility. "My questioning is good for you," he told the people in effect. "The doubts I raise are such as to strengthen the sinews of your minds. Athens needs me, and I intend to continue plaguing you with questions as I have always done." The huge jury thereupon found Socrates guilty as charged by a vote of 281 to 220. They might have reduced his sentence to something like banishment from Athens if Socrates had been willing to accept such punishment. But, as he told the jury, his own view was that Athens ought to honor and support him as a public benefactor. Offended by that seeming boast, the jury voted for imposing the death penalty.

His execution was delayed for some time by a sacred festival. During that period Socrates lay in jail and worked at setting some of Aesop's fables in verse form. He felt that he had slighted poetry somehow, and this seemed a good moment to make up for it. His jailers were bribed to let Socrates out. But, despite his friends' urging, the philosopher declined to escape. "In battle," he explained, "I never left the post to which my officers had assigned me. My present post has been assigned by God, and I will not leave it either." He spent his last day on earth conducting an inquiry with his friends. The subject of their final discussion together was, appropriately enough, the immortality of the soul. His arguments in favor of the idea were not wishful, but serene. At sunset the executioner brought in a potion of hemlock, deadly

poison, for Socrates to drink. His friends begged the philosopher to
wait a bit longer. The afterglow of the sun still lay upon Mount Hymet-
tus, they pointed out. But Socrates simply said a word or two of prayer
"for an auspicious journey hence," and drank the potion off. The afterglow of his own action is with us still.

Among Socrates' youngest disciples, toward the end, was a gallant
aristocrat named Xenophon. One day he came to Socrates in great excitement to report that he had been invited to join a Greek mercenary
force serving under a Persian satrap. Xenophon had been too young to
fight in the Peloponnesian War. Here was his chance to make his name
as a soldier. Should he take it? Socrates thought the best course would
be for Xenophon to consult the Delphic oracle. The young man did so,
but his question to the god concerned what sacrifices he should make
in order to assure success in his venture. As Socrates later pointed out to
him, that should have been the second question, not the first one.
Xenophon had set his mind in advance, which was not the spirit in
which to consult an oracle. But since the god had said which sacrifices
to make, he concluded, Xenophon had better go ahead as planned.

Xenophon marched with ten thousand Greek spearmen deep into
Asia. These mercenaries proved to be formidable on the battlefield.
But the satrap who employed them lost the war. A "peace conference"
followed, at which the Greek commanding officers were all murdered.
Surrounded by hostile forces, a thousand miles from home, the Greeks
elected new leaders, among them Xenophon. He led a long, long retreat northward from Mesopotamia over the snow-blocked Taurus
Mountains to the Black Sea, fighting most of the way. Xenophon later
wrote a full account of his exploit, called *Anabasis*. This was the first
true-life adventure yarn in literature, and it makes stirring reading still.

While Xenophon was performing wonders of heroism and re-
sourcefulness out East, Socrates suffered his martyrdom. Meanwhile,
another of Socrates' disciples, the young Plato, began to assert himself.
Before meeting Socrates, Plato had tried his hand at writing tragedies.
Now he wrote a delicate and dramatic monument to Socrates. The portrait was put in the form of a dialogue, and Plato made the happy
tragedy of his master's martyrdom play itself out in the reader's mind.
This, too, was an achievement absolutely new in literature. The basic
rule of fifth-century tragedy had been to portray a great man's doom as

brought about by some flaw in his character, and to purge the audience
with feelings of pity and terror. Plato reversed the form. He showed
his hero quite unflawed, going to meet destiny in a calm and cheerful
spirit. Instead of pity or terror, Plato's dialogues, such as *Apology,
Euthyphro, Crito, Phaedo,* and *Republic,* excite wondering admiration.

Plato is said to have been a broad, stoop-shouldered person, gentle,
and unadventurous except in the mind. But he faced a sharp crisis
while still a young man. Dionysius the Younger, the tyrant of Greek
Syracuse in Sicily, invited him to come and tutor the crown prince.
With Socrates dead, and Athens in a depressed, ugly mood, Plato was
glad to go. But he found the tyrant's court not to his liking. It was the
sort of place, he said, where one was expected to overeat twice daily
and never to sleep alone. Plato's outspoken strictures on Sicilian mate-
rialism exasperated Dionysius and, as the story goes, he presented
Plato to a Spartan who was sailing for home, with orders to dispose of
the puritanical young snob in any way which might appear appropriate.
The Spartan accordingly dropped Plato off, in chains, at the slave mar-

A Greek theater with stone bleachers carved out of a hillside at Syracuse

ket on the island of Aegina, close by the Piraeus on the Greek mainland.

Plato was lucky. A rich merchant of Cyrene in Libya bought him and instantly gave him his freedom. Plato had known the man before, and had taken pains to condemn his extravagant manner of life. Safe home in Athens once again, Plato raised his own purchase price among friends and offered it to his benefactor. But the man of Cyrene would not accept repayment, so Plato used the money to buy the Academus, a garden a mile west of Athens. There he built his "Academy," a school of metaphysical studies which was to survive for some nine hundred years until closed by Justinian in 529 A.D. The lintel over the front entrance carried the inscription "You cannot enter here unless you know geometry." Socrates would not have set even so slight a barrier in the path of a truth seeker. But Plato was a contemplative sort of man and he expected his own disciples to devote whole decades to purely intellectual research. His philosophy, he wrote, was "not a thing that can be put into words. Only from long discussion and musing upon the subject and from living together can it be communicated. Then, suddenly

like a flame leaping a gap, the light kindles in another person's soul—where it discovers its own nourishment." Metaphysics, for Plato, was a personal and communal pursuit. Its object seems to have been fundamentally religious: illumination of the individual soul. The same drive for spiritual illumination was to color Christianity in centuries to come. Many of the early Christian fathers read Plato. As for his intellectual influence upon the special problems of metaphysics, it was and is incalculable. As the modern philosopher Alfred North Whitehead put the case: "The safest general characterization of the European philosophical tradition is that it consists of a series of footnotes to Plato."

Some historians of the subject would amend that statement to include Aristotle's name as well. It is difficult to tell where Plato ends and Aristotle begins. There seem to be contradictions between the two, but these are perhaps more apparent than real. Aristotle studied for almost twenty years at Plato's feet. That very long apprenticeship is without parallel in the annals of original philosophy. How could a man possessing such tremendous power of intellect as Aristotle have been so patient a pupil? It may be that what Plato gave was not information or even methodology so much as it was spiritual communion. Plato died at his desk in the year 348 B.C., or thereabout. An amiable nephew succeeded him as head of the Academy. Aristotle, who was perhaps disappointed not to get that job, accepted an invitation from King Philip of Macedon. For some years he was tutor to Philip's brilliant and fiery son, Prince Alexander. When he returned to Athens, at about fifty years of age, it was to set up his own school, called the Lyceum.

Aristotle's writings which have come down to us consist of notes for lectures at the Lyceum. He put matters at his school on a less mystical and more scientific footing than prevailed at the Academy. His students worked together with him on wide-ranging projects in ethics, epistomology, natural history, aesthetics, political history, and criticism. Aristotle developed a passion for categorizing, classifying, and compiling. This has been the main thrust of intellectual investigation ever since. He had a genius for setting things in perspective. Here is one brief example. Aristotle once argued that the early Ionian philosophers such as Thales were concerned with material causes, the Pythagoreans with formal causes, Empedocles with efficient causes, and Socrates with final causes. When Thales said that everything began with

water, in other words, he was pointing to a material cause. When Pythagoras reduced the universe to numerical relationships, he was dealing with a formal cause. When Empedocles asserted that love and hate command the interaction of the elements, he was celebrating an efficient cause. Finally, when Socrates showed a way to live according to God's will, he was demonstrating faith in a final cause. There is nothing abstruse about such classifications as these; they have the virtue of clarifying abstruse matters.

Aristotle's most famous pupil, Alexander, once sent him the following note: "If you have made public what we have learnt from you, how shall we be any better than the rest? I myself would rather excel in learning than in riches or power." Aristotle wrote back and told the young prince not to worry. It was true, he admitted, that some Lyceum lectures were being made public. But no one could understand them unless, as in Alexander's own case, he had been given the secret keys to their significance.

The owl of Athena, wisdom's bird, flies only when the light begins to fade. This has been said about philosophy as well. At Athens, it is true, philosophy came into its own late in the day. Political life had diminished. The leaders now were not men of action but orators and champions of lost causes, such as Demosthenes and Isocrates. Demosthenes urged the Athenian Assembly, in vain most of the time, to make war against King Philip of Macedon. His lofty, fiery "Philippics," three political speeches on this subject, used to be required reading for aspiring statesmen. But the orator received more applause than cooperation and, though Athens did eventually go to war against Philip, Demosthenes himself exerted practically no effect upon the course of history. As for Isocrates, he counseled Athens to make peace with Philip. Isocrates hoped, vainly also, that Philip would lead all Greece in a holy war against the Persians. This was also met with indifference. Business was good. The slave trade remained brisk. Athenian manufactures were prized all around the Mediterranean. The unemployed could generally find work as mercenaries in distant armies. Mere dreams of glory glowed in the Athenian dusk. The rich got richer, and the poor poorer. The population of substantial citizens at Athens and elsewhere in Greece declined by about half in the hundred years following the Peloponnesian War.

Greek sculpture in better times had represented gods moving impassively upon some dimly understood but still eternal plane. The new master sculptors such as Praxiteles and Scopas were wont to represent passively beautiful bodies and strong human sentiments. There is a danger here of derogating what was still, by all accounts, miraculous work. The marble "Hermes" at Olympia is from Praxiteles' studio, and it may be a copy of a bronze from his own hand. The piece gives some idea of his extraordinary balance, sweetness, and subtlety. As for his long-lost "Aphrodite," which stood in the Greek colony of Cnidos in southwest Asia Minor, Romans used to make special sea journeys simply to look at it. This carving was the subject of a celebrated Greek epigram which might be translated:

> *Aphrodite blushed and said, "I protest!*
> *Praxiteles, when did you see me undressed?"*

The literature of the period, like its art, was somewhat more knowing than inspired. Prose dialogues, disquisitions, and orations of an exceedingly polished kind came into their own. However, the great dramatists and poets of the century before had not one worthy heir. The theater naturally kept on. But, like our own, it was dominated by star performers rather than poets. Revivals of the old tragedies, especially ones by Euripides, were frequent. The only fresh theatrical development was in the realm of polite social comedy. The gentle master of that art was named Menander. His few surviving works indicate that he must have been a kind of Praxiteles in verse. The rueful sweetness of the following lines sums up the spirit of Athens' twilight:

> *Think of this lifetime as a festival*
> *Or visit to a strange city, full of noise,*
> *Buying and selling, thieving, dicing-stalls*
> *And joy-parks. If you leave it early, friend,*
> *Why, think you have gone to find a better inn;*
> *You have paid your fare and leave no enemies.*
> *The lingerer tires, loses his fare, grows old,*
> *And lacks he knows not what: moons round and seeks*
> *To find an enemy and a plotting world,*
> *And no smooth passage when, in time, he goes!*

The Three Graces, *a copy of a Hellenistic work, executed in the third century* B.C. *at Cyrene, in Libya*

The times were decadent by comparison with what had gone before. Ares, the God of War "with his unseeing eyes set in a pig face," as Sophocles put it, ruled then as now. The rest of this chapter will have to do mainly with men of the sword.

Athens played no great part in what the new warriors did. She had reinstituted democracy, of a mercantile kind. But rich and practical Athenians, men of affairs, learned how to manipulate the voters by money. Bribery became commonplace. The speeches from the mouths of politicians were composed by highly paid professionals and public-relations experts. So, in a sense, Athens remained stable politically. The powerful lived in luxury while the poor were persuaded of their own freedom at least. The growing slave population exercised no overt influence on anything.

Sparta, meanwhile, was finding the fragments of Athens' shattered empire troublesome. The Spartans demanded tribute as the Athenians had done, but they gave nothing in return. Far from defending the Ionian city-states against Persia, for example, they sold them out to Artaxerxes II. Nearer home, in Boeotia, they used treachery to seize control of Thebes, which had been their staunchest ally. Naturally, they very soon made themselves more hated than the Athenians had been. In the year 379 B.C., the tide of Greek affairs began to turn against Sparta. The Spartan garrison at Thebes was overcome and the Spartans expelled. Thereafter, for some time, Thebes championed the ancient city-state ideals. A great Theban general named Pelopidas campaigned northward well into semibarbarous Macedon. (He brought a young prince, Philip of Macedon, home to Thebes as a hostage.)

More spectacularly successful still was a second hero of the new Thebes: Epaminondas. He marched right through the Peloponnesus to the sea, and freed the Messenians of Mount Ithome from Spartan domination. Epaminondas just missed sacking Sparta. He would have managed even that, but for the fact that Sparta's subject Helots chose —intriguingly enough—to defend their masters.

A Spartan force, well-bolstered with allies, threatened to take full revenge upon Thebes in the year 371 B.C. Epaminondas elected to meet it on the open plain, although his army was very much outnumbered. He massed his men into a new-style phalanx fifty shields deep. His shock troops at the front of the phalanx comprised a so-called "Sacred

Band" of soldier-artistocrats pledged to fight to the death. He moved his massed spearmen obliquely, in a compact body, against the traditionally stretched-out battle line of the Spartans—a vulnerable twelve shields deep: Epaminondas crashed right through it. Of seven hundred Spartan hoplites engaged in the fight, four hundred were killed in the Battle of Leuctra, as it came to be known. With that, Epaminondas destroyed the last vestige of the old legend concerning Spartan invincibility. At the same time, he taught ten-year-old Prince Philip of Macedon an unforgettable lesson in tactics.

A dozen years later, the prince, who had returned home, mounted the Macedonian throne. Philip's country was very poor and under constant threat from all directions. His people, however, were hard-muscled mountaineers, and loyal monarchists. Philip proceeded to shape them into an armed camp which could defy the entire known world.

Philip's chief weapon was the phalanx which he had seen developed at Thebes. His own innovation was to lengthen the spears of his men. Perhaps the new Macedonian lances were supported by shoulder straps as well as by the hands of the warriors. Modern estimates of their length range from thirteen to twenty feet. Philip's first conquests, eastward in Thrace, included gold mines necessary to finance his army. His next, southward in Thessaly, provided him with cavalry recruits who proved essential adjuncts to the Macedonian phalanx. Philip also adopted the new Persian tactic of financing various city-states to go to war against each other. He used his own army only when necessary and when he could be reasonably certain of victory. One day in the year 356 B.C., he got three pieces of good news. His best general, Parmenion, had decisively beaten the barbarian Illyrians to the north of Macedon. His chariot team had come in first in the Olympian Games. And finally his queen, Olympias, had given birth to a son.

Despite these good omens, the Greeks continued to look down on Macedon. Its monarchical form of government appeared old-fashioned to them. The Macedonians claimed descent from the Greek hero Achilles, and from the demigod Heracles. They spoke a dialect of Greek, but it was a far cry from the polished accents of Athens. Their prowess as warriors was not to be ignored, but it failed to justify their abrasive arrogance. So Philip's claim to be the protector of Greece, and the chief arbiter of quarrels between the city-states, was disputed.

At Chaeronea, in the year 338 B.C., the combined armies of Athens and Thebes offered challenge to Philip. A marble lion, with its legs clumsily restored, still marks the place where the battle centered. The victory there was won by a cavalry charge under the command of Alexander, now eighteen years old. Greece having been subdued, Philip turned his attention to Asia. Isocrates of Athens had been urging him to annex Anatolia at least, and this advice made good sense to the king. Philip was in his forties, an imperious and shrewd monarch with a weakness for women and wine. He had already put away Alexander's mother, Olympias, in order to marry a second queen.

Philip consulted the Delphic oracle concerning the campaign which he had planned. "The bull is garlanded," Apollo told him. "The sacrificer is ready; the consummation is at hand." Philip assumed that the bull of the prophecy signified the Persian monarchy. However that may have been, he himself met his end within a few months. While celebrating a daughter's wedding, he was struck down by an assassin. His bodyguards instantly killed the man, and so the motives of the murder were never known. But the suspicion was, and is, that jealous and rejected Queen Olympias was somehow involved. The year was 336 B.C.

Alexander, who was twenty, instantly ascended the throne of Macedon. Northern invaders challenged him. He and his superb standing army dealt with them. Demosthenes at Athens was saying, however, that Alexander seemed to be "merely a crazy boy." The Greeks in general took arms against the continued authority of Macedon. Thebes led the revolt.

Alexander marched south and razed Thebes to the ground. He spared her temples only, together with a single house which was said to have been the residence of the poet Pindar. He sold the whole surviving population of Thebes into slavery. Then, having cowed the Greeks at his back, he crossed the Hellespont with more than thirty thousand infantry and five thousand cavalry. About a quarter of his force was Macedonian. The rest were mainly Greeks and semisavages of the northern mountains. His entourage included engineers, geographers, botanists, and a court historian named Callisthenes, who was Aristotle's nephew, for Alexander intended his expedition to be scientific as well as military. His first stop on the Asiatic continent was at Troy.

Like Xerxes before him, Alexander offered sacrifices there. Xerxes

had solemnly sworn to avenge the sacking of Troy. Alexander now swore to avenge Xerxes' own invasion. As Achilles had done, he held athletic contests on the Trojan Plain. In the local temple he came upon a shield which was said to belong to Achilles and he appropriated this, leaving his own shield in its place.

Now he declared Troy to be free of Persian domination and a Greek city-state in its own right. Ironically, Greek mercenaries in the pay of the Persian satrap Spithridates were massing against him. At a stream called the Granicus, Spithridates tried to halt Alexander's advance. Acting against the advice of his father's old general, Parmenion, Alexander stormed across the river. The air was alive with arrows shot by the famous archers of Persia, and the Greek mercenaries in the Persian ranks stood firm on the high ground. Alexander's troops were, however, superior. Riding his great charger Bucephalus, the Macedonian king personally led the attack. The Persian commander met him in the midst of the melee and came very close to splitting open Alexander's head with his war-axe. The commander of the Macedonian cavalry guard, Clitus the Black, barely saved Alexander by hacking away Spithridates' arm. At that point the Persians broke and ran. Alexander had no opportunity to pursue them because the Greek mercenary contingents of the enemy fought on. After a hard struggle, he captured some two thousand of them. These he sent back to Macedon in chains. He stripped three hundred splendid suits of armor from the enemy dead. The armor he dispatched to Athens as an offering to the goddess Athena, whose temple Xerxes had long ago violated. The Hellespont, Ionia, and the eastern half of Anatolia were now in Alexander's hands. But the Persian navy with its Phoenician allies commanded the sea. In this position the shrewdest policy, which Parmenion and other generals urged, might well have been consolidation. Alexander had a different idea. He proposed to destroy Persian sea power on land, by marching right around the "golden crescent" to Egypt and capturing every enemy port along the way.

Before starting southward, Alexander paused at the ancient Phrygian capital of Gordium. The temple there contained a complex knot whose ends were well concealed within the mesh. Tradition held that whoever could untie this knot would rule Asia. Alexander, so the story goes, simply sliced the thing in half with one stroke of his sword. That

may be a legend, but it suits Alexander's character as well as his instinct for dramatically symbolic acts.

In the year 333 B.C., as Alexander was descending upon Syria, Darius III, the Great King of Persia, moved to cut him off from the rear. This was what Alexander had been hoping for. Darius had with him about the same number of troops and cavalry as did Alexander. But, as the young king told his officers, Xenophon's experience had shown that Greeks were better fighters than the Persians. Xenophon, after all, had led ten thousand Greek spearmen unscathed out of Persia. "Sleep well," Alexander added. "In the morning we'll strike north and meet Darius at Issus." He proved to be a true prophet. At Issus the Macedonian cavalry, led by Alexander astride Bucephalus, broke the Persian line. Darius barely escaped, and the Great King's mother, wife, and two daughters were captured. His war treasury at Damascus passed into Alexander's hands. Chastened, the Great King wrote a letter offering to cede the western third of his empire to Alexander. He proposed to make the Euphrates River their mutual border. The suggestion appeared generous in the extreme, but Alexander turned it down. His

A Roman mosaic from the first century A.D. *depicts a fearless Alexander astride his steed Bucephalus at the battle of Issus.*

long reply to Darius' letter was an astonishing mixture of youthful braggadocio and lofty scorn. It concluded:

"Come here. If you are afraid that I might receive you ungraciously, then send a few friends first to try me out. When you yourself come, you may ask for the return of your mother, wife, and children. Whatever else you can persuade me to give, you shall have. But in the future you must address me as Supreme Lord of all Asia. Do not presume again to communicate on equal terms. Just tell me, as the possessor of everything you have, what you may need. Otherwise I shall take steps to treat you as a miscreant. If you claim your kingdom, stand and fight for it. There is no earthly use in your attempting escape, for I shall pursue wherever you go."

Meanwhile a single Syrian city chose to hold out against Alexander. Tyre was a remarkably well-walled island town just off the shore. It sheltered a fine harbor on the seaward side, within the walls. Because Persia still held command of the sea, Tyre appeared impregnable. Its position was rather like that of Athens during the first decades of the Peloponnesian War. Alexander's whole plan of world conquest, if that is what he really had in mind, was in danger of foundering upon this single stumbling block. He spent most of the year 332 B.C. besieging the city. His engineers built a broad causeway out to the island, and laid out tracks along which they advanced armored towers against the city's walls. But the men of Tyre burned those towers by running fire ships against them in a brilliant night sortie. Sidon and other Syrian ports, however, capitulated to Alexander. Using their ships, he was able to blockade Tyre. After seven months of supremely gallant resistance, Tyre fell. About eight thousand of its citizens were massacred by Alexander's troops. Alexander ordered one of his catapults to be wheeled into the local temple of Heracles and left there as an offering to the demigod, his distant ancestor.

With Tyre destroyed at last, Alexander headed southward again. At Gaza, on the edge of the Sinai Desert, he faced another desperate struggle. Alexander was wounded in the shoulder by catapult fire from the city's walls. He was compelled to send back to Tyre for his siege engines. Using these, Alexander finally battered down Gaza's defenses. The Arabian garrison was slaughtered. All the women and children were sold into slavery. War, as practiced in Alexander's time, was a

more cruel, complex, and elaborate exercise than romantic legends may indicate. Ruthlessness was a form of insurance for the victors. Losers often lost everything.

In seven days, Alexander crossed the desert to the Nile Delta. The Egyptians naturally knew of his accomplishments. They were also aware of how he punished resistance. So Alexander found himself received at Memphis, the Egyptian capital, with flowers and loud priestly chants of acclaim. He was the savior of Egypt, her legitimate Pharaoh, without striking a blow. On a reef-sheltered shore beside Lake Mariotes in the Delta, Alexander founded the first of seventy cities named after himself. This first Alexandria would prove to be his finest and most lasting monument. It was laid out by architects and engineers detached for the purpose from the young king's personal entourage. Dinocrates, the chief planner, designed straight avenues and streets in rigidly rectangular blocks, like modern New York. He connected the new city with an inshore island by means of a long bridge supported on arches. This more than doubled the available waterfront of Alexandria's twin harbors. The city was to be the Port Said of its day, connected by the Nile and an east–west canal to the Red Sea. Moreover, it would prove to be the main fountainhead of Hellenistic—Greek oriented—culture for century after century.

From the site of Alexandria, the twenty-five-year-old conqueror struck westward toward Libya with a small force. His intention did not become clear until he turned southward into the desert. He was making for the distant oasis of Ammon, which is now known as Siwa. There were no tracks across the drifting dunes; Alexander's guides soon lost their way. Thirst attacked the army, but the men were saved by a totally unexpected fall of rain. We have the word of one of Alexander's generals, named Ptolemy, that a pair of serpents appeared and guided them at last to the safety of the oasis itself. Why had Alexander brought his men through such desperate natural hazards to this faraway date garden? Not for conquest, it turned out, but only to consult the local oracle of the Egyptian god Ammon. To Alexander's mind, Ammon and the Greek god Zeus were one and the same. He wished to learn something secret, personal, and important. No man knows what his question to the oracle was. But it is said that Ammon, or Zeus, speaking through a golden mask, hailed Alexander as his own dear

Views of a veiled dancer, cast in bronze around 200 B.C. at Alexandria, in Egypt

son. One thing is certain, namely that Alexander sent a letter to his mother concerning the oracle. He told her that the god had said something for her ears alone which could not be written down. Alexander promised to whisper this message to her upon returning home. In fact he was never to see Macedon again.

Egypt having been secured, Alexander now struck eastward into the Mesopotamian heartland. He crossed the Euphrates and the Tigris. At Gaugamela, near the ruins of Assyrian Nineveh, Darius challenged him a second time. The new Persian forces included far more cavalry than Alexander's did. Moreover, fifteen war elephants from India and two hundred chariots equipped with whirling scythes gave Darius an added advantage of strangeness and surprise. Faced with so bristling a host, Alexander was cautious. He brought his own army to a halt almost within sight of the Persians, and camped for the night. Parmenion urged a night attack, on the grounds that darkness and confusion might somewhat equalize the two armies. Perhaps the Persians would panic upon being routed out of bed. But Alexander replied that he had no wish to steal a victory like a thief. When morning came, he maneuvered his troops in precise and rather razzle-dazzle fashion to bemuse the waiting Persians. Stumbling over themselves in their efforts to parry Alexander's light thrusts, the forces of Darius split for a moment. Alexander led his cavalry thunderously into the narrow gap between the Persian ranks. Darius himself was put in grave danger by this desperate onslaught, and once again he fled the battlefield. The struggle then changed character; it became a slaughter. All day, Alexander's men pursued their enemy across the plain, cutting down the Persians as they ran.

Babylon, by far the greatest city in the world at that time, was Alexander's next objective. The Babylonian governor, Mazaeus, welcomed the conqueror at the gates. Alexander accepted Mazaeus' switch of allegiance from Darius to himself, and he graciously confirmed the governor in power. The only considerable changes which Alexander made in the Babylonian administration were first to appoint a Macedonian defense minister, and secondly to appropriate the rich gleanings of the tax structure. Resting at Babylon, he decided to make the city the capital of his whole empire. Meanwhile he amused himself by hunting lions in parks set aside for that purpose.

Elephants, like the one saddled with a warrior's perch in this drawing, were used by Eastern potentates in combat against Alexander's armies.

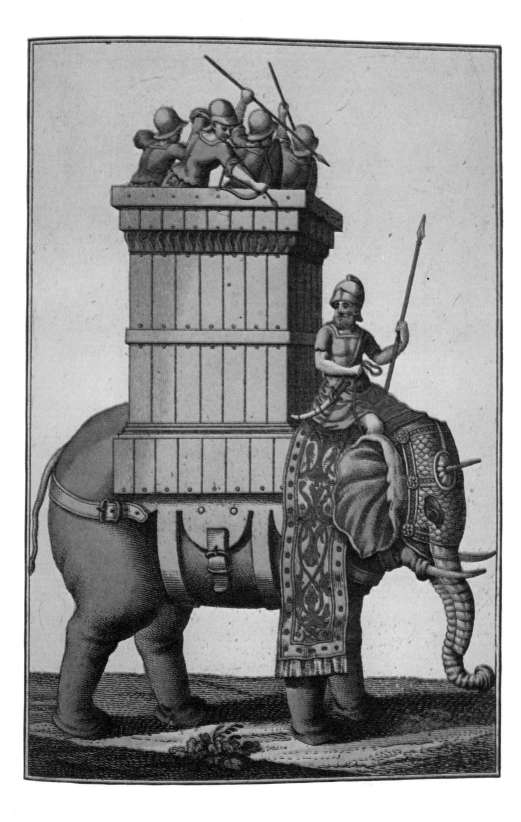

Word spread that Alexander's troops had been more than half conquered by the wine, women, and soft hospitality of Babylon. Grimly, Alexander did all he could to encourage that rumor. Then, after a mere six weeks, he suddenly marched out to the southeast with all of his fattened-up, pleasure-weary veterans. He led them through snowy passes of winter, and the harassments of hostile tribes, to seize the legendary capitals of Persia one by one. These were Susa, Persepolis, and Ecbatana. At all three places, he captured immense treasuries of gold. Alexander ordered that they be minted into coins, which he then freely spent. Croesus had never been so rich as this. Alexander deliberately transformed the whole economy of the Middle East from a conservative agricultural basis to one of war and feverish business enterprise. His inflationary measures may have done more than any other factor to spread the restless Greek spirit abroad.

Darius had been pushed all the way back to his easternmost province, and Alexander pursued him even there. Bessus, the governor of Bactria, thought to please Alexander by assassinating the unhappy emperor. But instead, Alexander was enraged to be robbed of his noble prize. He eventually captured Bessus, and submitted the man to ignominy, torture, and execution as a renegade. Alexander himself now claimed the title of Great King, and he wished to make very plain the terrible authority of his position.

Unlike his father Philip, Alexander had never been at all susceptible to women. He used to say that sex and sleep alike reminded him unpleasantly of his own mortal condition. But now, whether it was for purposes of policy or whether he was growing lonely in his power, he married a Bactrian princess named Roxana. Under her influence, it may have been, he took to wearing the loose tunic and baggy trousers which were Persian costume. He campaigned northeast through the Hindu Kush mountain range into Samarkand; his battle lust was still undiminished. But now for the first time he, like his father, fell prey to wine. At a court banquet one night Clitus the Black, the commander of Alexander's cavalry, taunted the Great King with having forgotten his Macedonian origin and even his common humanity. "This hand," Clitus shouted, waving his right fist, "was all that saved you, Alexander, at the River Granicus." Drunk, and red with rage, Alexander tried to strike his old friend. Other officers forcibly held him back. Alexan-

der then shouted for his bodyguards, but they refused to intervene. General Ptolemy hustled Clitus out of the room. Moments later Clitus reappeared at another door, laughing and shouting: "I am here!" Alexander seized a spear, flung it, and transfixed his lifelong friend.

Of course he suffered agonies of remorse. Advisers comforted him somewhat with the ancient argument that a Great King can do no wrong. But certain officers conspired against Alexander's life. Among them was the son of faithful General Parmenion. Alexander had the conspirators executed. At the same time, for safety's sake, he arranged for Parmenion to be murdered. He had also to deal with a conspiracy among the page boys, and had some of them killed. For good measure, he imprisoned their tutor. This was none other than the historian Callisthenes, who died, apparently in his close captivity.

Alexander, putting his troubles behind him, stormed over the Khyber Pass into what is now northern India. His nearly suicidal courage in battle together with his constant willingness to dare the seemingly impossible inspired his veterans anew. Yet it also brought them near to despair. In a major engagement for control of Taxila and the Indus River, Alexander barely defeated the Punjab monarch named Paurava (or, in the Greek, Porus). Paurava had two hundred war elephants in his cavalry. As Alexander advanced against the trumpeting grey wall, his old horse, Bucephalus, died. Bucephalus was buried on the battlefield. His name and fame are still revered in that part of the world.

Paurava proved to be just as dignified in defeat as he had been formidable in battle. "How should I treat you?" Alexander asked him. "As a king," Paurava replied. Alexander thereupon made an ally of him. Their battle marked the limit of Alexander's eastward plunge. It occurred at the Hydaspes (the present-day Jhelum) River in the year 326 B.C., when Alexander was thirty. His troops refused to go any farther. Perhaps Alexander in his proud heart agreed with them that the time had now come to head westward again. He had hoped to reach the eastern edge of civilization, and an encircling ocean shore. As an explorer, he might have done so, but now he saw that it could not be accomplished with sword in hand. Further kingdoms—great ones—lay beyond in India, as Paurava told him. The armies of those countries, it was said, deployed war elephants not by hundreds but by thousands. In the jungles of India, even an Alexander might sink and disappear.

Some Hindu holy men of Taxila also helped shake Alexander's iron resolve. He could not help admiring their self-sufficiency. They went stark naked, and they used to stand on one leg meditating for hours upon end. "You, oh king," they are said to have told him, "are roaming far from home. Your spirit is troubled, and you appear determined to trouble the whole world. But it all comes to one thing in the end." Alexander managed to persuade one of these ascetics, whose name was Calanus, to accompany him home to the West. The other holy men thought Calanus a fool to go. The conqueror, however, had struck a chord of brotherhood in Calanus. Like Alexander, he was curious.

Would it be possible to open a sea route from East to West? To find this out, Alexander now built a flotilla consisting of no less than a

A grief-stricken Olympias falls on Alexander's bier, as mourners cry out, in this medieval Persian miniature.

thousand ships on the Hydaspes River. He dropped down the Hydaspes to the Indus, and thence to the Indian Ocean, fighting much of the way. The mud-walled cities of the Brahmans resisted him to the last. Storming the walls of one of them, Alexander led the way up a scaling ladder, followed by his shield-bearer and two other men. As those four leaped inside the battlements, the ladder was hurled down. Alexander and his companions fought for their lives against the whole city until the Macedonians succeeded in battering through the gates below. The conqueror was severely wounded. His comrades carried him from the city on his shield. Yet within a few days he walked again. Alexander had often suffered battle wounds. Nothing on earth, apparently, could keep him down for long. Glory was no mere attribute of this man but an intrinsic—perhaps a healing—quality; and willpower was his stock in trade.

He showed this once again during his march along the desert coast from the mouth of the Indus back to the Persian Gulf. Alexander intended to dig wells and cache supplies for his fleet during the course of this march. He had no conception of the forces of nature opposing him. The Gedrosian Desert proved to be so hot that his army could only march at night. They lost their way now and again, between the blazing constellations and the dunes. Bedouins picked off all stragglers. One day a downpour flooded a dry wadi where the army lay encamped, and drowned a third of his men. The next day, as before, there was practically no water. A helmetful of water became as precious as all the gold of Susa and Persepolis. A few drops, which might or might not be discovered at the next tiny oasis, were all that stood between each man and death. At one stop, barely a cupful was found. They brought it to Alexander. Without so much as wetting his lips, he deliberately poured it out upon the sand before the eyes of his troops. Choking with thirst though they were, the men cheered and struggled on. The march took sixty days in all, and it consumed some thirty thousand of Alexander's best men. Yet at the end, he rendezvoused with his fleet successfully.

His ships also had encountered trouble, though it was nothing like what the army went through. Mediterraneans all, the sailors were astonished and baffled by the force of the Indian Ocean's tides. At one point a large herd of whales bore down upon the ships, spouting irridescent geysers as they came. The men had never imagined the exis-

tence of such creatures. The fleet fell into confusion as the sailors dropped their oars. But luckily its commander, Nearchus of Crete, had the presence of mind to order battle stations manned at once and every bugle blown full blast, and the whales vanished.

Among Alexander's surviving friends was Calanus the holy man. Now safely arrived at Susa, he fell sick. This had never happened to him before. Calanus quietly refused medical care. He asked that a pyre be built upon which he might immolate himself. Alexander tried in vain to persuade Calanus to go on living. Failing in that attempt, he ordered full military honors for his friend. Calanus was garlanded like a sacrifice and led to the pyre. He distributed to the crowd the precious incense which had been consigned to burn with him. To Alexander, Calanus said simply: "We meet again at Babylon." Then the impassive ascetic gave himself to the flames. Perhaps the grosser, fiercer side of Alexander burned away with the passing of Calanus. At thirty-two, he looked back upon his far-flung battles as the natural extravagances of youth. His new aim was not to win the world for Hellenic ideals, nor was it for personal rule. Now he longed for nothing less than the reconciliation of East and West. As a small step in that direction, he himself took a second wife. She was a daughter of Darius, named Barsine.

Feeling, perhaps, that bedroom battles beat international conflict, Alexander went on to marry ten thousand of his finest men to Persian girls whom he provided with generous dowries. Finally, he enlisted thirty thousand Persian youths among his Macedonian troops. He sent back word to the Greek city-states that he was now a god in whose honor they ought to reconcile their differences. To his army, Alexander announced that the veterans of his ten-year campaign in Asia were no longer needed. Let each one retire, he said, with an immense bonus and glorious memories. To Alexander's absolute disgust, the troops rebelled at this. The Macedonians cried out that they would all go, to a man, since Alexander had turned against them. He was Persian now in all but name, they complained. Alexander, furious, retired to his tent and sulked—like Achilles at the siege of Troy. After three days, he began summoning in Asiatic noncoms and promoting them to positions over his Macedonians. With that, former companions crowded around his tent in tears. They had not really meant to leave him in the lurch, they explained, but only to let him know that they loved him

just as much as did the Persians. His Macedonian officers begged that they be allowed to kiss him as the Persian custom was, and be accepted again as his kinsmen. Alexander was mollified. He stepped out of his tent. "But you are *all* my kinsmen," he shouted. The whole host, united again, sang their victory hymn.

Alexander planned an exploratory naval expedition from the Persian Gulf down around the coast of Arabia to the Red Sea and Egypt. He intended to forge a chain of water commerce from Babylon to Alexandria. This would have assured the Hellenization of southern Arabia and East Africa. But the one man with sufficient imagination and force of personality to bring it about fell ill, one fine evening, at a party in Babylon. Medical men have guessed that Alexander was brought low by a malaria-carrying mosquito.

Alexander could have created something larger than empire—a peaceful cosmopolis—if he had lived. So some historians maintain, at least. Even at this present distance, it seems, Alexander commands deep loyalties. He left only one son, a child still in Roxana's womb, and doomed to assassination before very long. His generals kneeling by the deathbed begged: "To whom do you bequeath what you have got?" With his last breath, Alexander responded: "To the strongest."

His chief commanders carved the empire up. Egypt fell to General Ptolemy, who also had the wit to kidnap Alexander's body. Embalmers brought the corpse to Memphis in Egypt, where they restored it according to their art. The body was now fit to survive for centuries. It had been destined, according to Alexander's own wish, for final entombment in the western desert oasis of Ammon. Ptolemy thought, with reason, that it would be wasted there. Not many travelers got that far. So he built a splendid mausoleum at the crossroads of his own raw capital, Alexandria. Within the mausoleum, on permanent exhibition, he placed a crystal coffin. Inside the coffin, Alexander lay for all to see. Like Lenin in the Kremlin today, the hero stayed there perforce as a sort of tutelary deity composed of beeswax, cosmetics, and human clay.

Living, he had brought many people to death. Half a million ghosts, perhaps, convened to curse this pagan king on the far bank of the Styx. Alexander's whole adventure had been as sharp as vinegar—but also sweeter than the honeycomb. The afterglow of the glory that was Greece achieved its widest reach with him.

CHAPTER VI

THE BRIDGE
OF CHRIST

Alexander had shifted the Hellenic center of gravity right out of Greece itself. And for some generations after his death it stood at Alexandria, where General Ptolemy proved the strongest among Alexander's successors. His slice of the empire grew to include Libya to the west, Palestine to the east, and the island of Cyprus in the north.

The delta seacoast is low in profile and its waters are treacherously shallow. To overcome this drawback and make Alexandria the world's most important harbor, Ptolemy Soter ("Savior" as he now styled himself) built a lighthouse. This creation soon became, like the Hanging Gardens of Babylon, an object of wonder to travelers the world over. It was reputed to be four hundred feet in height. The illumination provided by the tall flaming wicks of its oil lamps was magnified and beamed far out to sea by means of reflecting mirrors. Greek science came together with Greek adventurousness in that monument. It was a practical thing, of course, but also a symbol of the ancient impulse which had drawn legendary Odysseus over the seas to the underworld and home again.

The world's first museum, or "home of the muses," was Ptolemy

Pyrrhus, king of Epirus and winner of a costly victory over Rome

Soter's second great contribution to civilization. In the beginning, he modeled it upon the Athenian Lyceum founded by Alexander's teacher, Aristotle. But that had been a relatively tiny and private institution whereas this one was immense and supported by Ptolemy's own almost bottomless tax resources.

Blessed with invariable sunshine, Egypt's fields were enriched each year by brown silt brought down upon the back of generous Nile. The great river was to prove faithful in this way for more than two thousand years to come. (Not until our own time was its nourishing force transposed to a different dimension, namely electric power, by the building of the Aswan Dam.) In classical times, Alexandria was the funnel for a major portion of the world's grain. Greece, which has so little arable land, obtained her bread chiefly from Egypt and only secondarily from Greek colonies along the Black Sea coast in southern Russia. All this being true, Ptolemy held in his fist at Alexandria an exceedingly rich and unfailing revenue. It enabled him to overshadow Alexander's other heirs in the military sense and at the same time to devote Alexandria to cultural pursuits. Alexandria never had anything like the spirit and creative drive of Athens in the age of Pericles, but she was vastly richer and more stable than her cultural ancestor.

At Alexandria the time of the textbook began. The museum there was the world's Oxford University, Ford Foundation, and Rand Corporation all rolled into one. Its highest functionary, traditionally, was a literary man. But at Alexandria the profession of literature ceased to be inspired. Grammarians took over. They laid down rules for such things as spelling and the use of accents. Those rules very soon assumed an importance quite out of proportion to their usefulness, which obtains to this day. As an example of the donnish dryness which threatened to bury Greek culture while presuming to preserve it, here is a communication from King Philadelphus (Ptolemy II) to the scholar Sosibius, who had complained that his salary was late in coming. "The first syllable of your name," the king replied, "occurs in Soter. The second occurs in Sosigenes, the third in Bion and the fourth in Apollonius. Since I have paid all four of those gentlemen, you may consider that you also have received your fee."

Government-sponsored scholarship and research exhibited the same strengths and the same drawbacks which it has today. As in the United

States and the Soviet Union now, Alexandrian scientists found themselves showered with funds but at the same time called upon to pursue nonhumanitarian lines of investigation. The affair of Queen Berenice's Hair may be taken as a case in point. Berenice, the wife of Ptolemy III, dedicated a lock of her hair in an Alexandrian temple. Unaccountably, it disappeared. The palace ordered the museum to get up a full report on the case. After a great deal of diligent digging and pondering in committee, the museum returned its verdict in verse form. Its conclusion was that Berenice's Hair had been translated to heaven as a constellation—which carries her name even now.

When Berenice's little daughter died, the palace decreed a leap year in her honor, to recur at regular four-year intervals. This brought solar and lunar calendars into harmony at long last. Once learned, the lesson was not forgotten. Our own "Julian" calendar is the Alexandrian one, which Julius Caesar saw fit to impose upon the world.

The work of the museum might be frivolous, as in the little business of Berenice's Hair, or practical, as in the institution of leap year. Then, too, it might be "pure" in the modern scientific sense of that term. Aristarchus of Samos was a museum member whose thoughts ranged very far. He submitted a paper to the Ptolemies arguing that the earth revolves around the sun. This paper apparently failed to convince them. The world was going to have to wait until the Renaissance to learn from the lips of Copernicus what Aristarchus had already guessed.

Eratosthenes held the museum's chief post—that of librarian—in Aristarchus' time. He used his intellectual and administrative powers to produce the world's first comprehensive geography. His maps were limited by the primitive state of exploration in his time, but they fitted the facts then known. There was nothing wishful or fabulous about Eratosthenes' map making. Yet he exercised the boldness of speculative science at its best. His greatest achievement had to do with measurement. At midday in midsummer at Alexandria, the sun casts a shadow of seven and a half degrees, or one fiftieth of a complete circle. Five hundred miles up the Nile, at Aswan, the sun casts no shadow at all during that singular midsummer moment. Therefore, said Eratosthenes, the earth must be fifty times five hundred miles (or 25,000 miles) around. He then proceeded to calculate the planet's diameter at 7,850 miles—a scant seventy-five miles off the true figure.

Such calculations were made possible by the greatest museum man of them all, Euclid. He dared tell a Ptolemy that "there is no royal road to geometry." The king seems to have taken this assertion in good part, but schoolchildren ever since have had cause to shudder at its grim truth. Euclid's *Elements* remained the mathematician's Bible until just the other day. In terrestrial conditions and at ordinary speeds it still works perfectly. Only deep space conditions and added dimensions put a wobble in Euclid's monument of the mind.

Now, let us come out of the museum and leave Egypt altogether. The year is 280 B.C., and mainland Greece stands once again under terrible threat. Two centuries previous, in the year 480, Xerxes had led his vast Asiatic host down upon Greece. The steadfastness of a Leonidas, the mother-wit of a Themistocles, and seeming miracles as well, were needed to hurl Xerxes back. This time the danger appeared just as great. Barbarian hordes of Gauls from the Danube region were marching through the mountains into Macedon. The country which had given birth to Alexander and his invincible spearmen was crumpling under the weight of barbarian battle-axes. The city-states of central Greece and the Peloponnesus banded together to try to stop the onrush of the Gallic host at Thermopylae. Brennus, the Gallic king, like Xerxes before him, detoured around the pass. But he did not bother to turn and destroy Thermopylae's defenders as Xerxes had done. Instead, he plunged straight on toward Delphi with his huge host. The allied Greek armies disbanded, because resistance appeared useless. Each city-state hoped privately to wait out and perhaps escape the Gallic sweep.

Brennus had heard that Delphi was filled with votive offerings of gold. Like Alexander bearing down upon Persian Persepolis with its treasury of gold bullion, Brennus came on fast. The priests at Delphi begged the god Apollo for some word. "What should we do?" they asked the oracle. A scorched-earth policy had been proposed by some. If the barbarians found no food and wine to sustain their advance, perhaps they might turn back. Such was the forlorn hope of the Greeks. They began removing their stores to mountain caves. But, strangely enough, the god vetoed this course. Let the barbarians come, the oracle commanded in Apollo's name. "The care for these things falls on me and the white maidens."

The only weakness of the fur-clad Gallic horde was its indiscipline.

A section from an Alexandrian astronomical treatise, written on papyrus, demonstrates the movements of the planets.

Brennus' army advanced raggedly. Contingents kept splitting off from the main body to pillage farms and villages along the way. Such detours would end with orgies of feasting and drunkenness, which put the horde in further disarray. Meanwhile a few thousand Greek warriors— no more than that—elected to help Apollo defend his sanctuary. Heroically, they stood up to King Brennus' initial attack along the Sacred Way. The earth quaked, according to contemporary accounts, and at the height of the battle Zeus rained thunderbolts upon the enemy. The priests of the shrine were shouting that they could see Apollo himself leading the fight and that they heard the twanging of his silver bow. One thing certain is that King Brennus was successfully beaten back. Perhaps only the vanguard of his horde had taken part.

At any rate, Brennus retired for the night and camped with all his hundreds of thousands in the deep gorge below the shrine. Then came the "white maidens" mentioned in Apollo's prophecy. The snow fell more and more thickly. Howling winds swept it into drifts around the sleeping Gauls. They woke up shivering. The dawn seemed only a lighter darkness to them. The whirling silent snow still fell blindingly upon them, blocking the gorge where they stood. Trying to climb up out of it toward the sanctuary, they slipped and fell. Clutching their battle-axes, they rolled down the slope. The Greek defenders of the shrine came after them, on the attack. Bewildered, the barbarians broke and ran this way and that. They called to one another through the snow, but soon lost touch. In small groups they wandered the frigid flank of Apollo's mountain. The villagers whose houses they had burned now appeared out of the snow with sharp pitchforks and pruning hooks. The Gauls ran, slipping and sliding, until struck down. Brennus himself was severely wounded. His bodyguard carried him on his shield down to a valley filled with sunshine, and then northward again toward home. Of the whole horde, perhaps a third got out of Greece alive. The god Apollo had been vindicated. At the same time, a new alarm had been sounded. From this point onward, for a thousand years and more, the main threats to civilization would spring from the fields and forests of the barbarian north.

Pyrrhus, a cousin of Alexander the Great, had inherited the northwesterly corner of Alexander's empire; namely, rugged Epirus along the coast of what is now Albania. Pyrrhus was a brilliant general, by all

accounts. His mountain troops were hard-bitten men. He might conceivably have stood up to the barbarian horde, but during the year 280 B.C., Pyrrhus was away in southern Italy. His purpose there was to save the city-states of Magna Grecia from the swelling power of republican Rome. Pyrrhus hoped that in so doing he could also carve out an overseas empire for himself with Tarantum (modern Taranto under the heel of the Italian boot) as its capital. The Romans had more reserves of manpower, by far, than Pyrrhus could command. He thought to overcome them by superior tactics and discipline. He brought war elephants along to overawe the Roman cavalry. But when Pyrrhus first looked down from a spur of the Apennines upon an armed camp of the Romans, he was appalled. There was nothing barbarous, he saw, about those four-square fortifications and those heavily armored troops drilling in the hot sun below. Pyrrhus did manage to win his first battles against the Romans, but only at an insupportable cost in blood. "One more such victory," he groaned, "and we are lost." The phrase "a Pyrrhic victory" passed into literature from that complaint. He retreated at last to the Epirus, in northwestern Greece, remarking that he was leaving a marvelous battlefield to Rome and Carthage.

Pyrrhus proved right. The Greek city-states of southern Italy and Sicily were swallowed up in the long Punic Wars between Rome and Carthage. Macedon joined the losing side in that struggle, and suffered severe defeat at Roman hands. Sparta, however, had made an alliance with the Roman Republic. The ancient Spartan ideals and the new Roman ones were not, after all, so far apart.

In times gone by, Greek intellectuals often had been impressed and even seduced by the puritanical virtues of Sparta. Now, in the same way, some of them were drawn to Rome. The historian Polybius first entered Rome as a Greek hostage, but he stayed to become the Republic's best political apologist and a tutor to Scipio Africanus. "To my thinking," Polybius wrote, "the greatest difference between the Roman Constitution and all others is in the sphere of religion. Everywhere else, religious feeling is regarded as superstition and a matter for reproach, but here it is the mortar which binds the whole state together." But, he concluded, Rome also was sure to degenerate in the course of time.

Polybius watched the burning of Carthage at Scipio's side. By the light of the blaze, he saw that tears were streaking the Roman victor's

cheeks. "Why do you weep?" he asked. Scipio replied with two lines from Homer's *Iliad*:

> *The day will come when holy Troy shall be destroyed,*
> *And Priam of the mighty spear, and Priam's tribe.*

The implication was obvious. Troy had risen and gone. So had the power of Nineveh and Babylon. Persia had flourished, only to see power fade away. In days gone by, Xerxes, the Persian Great King, had wept to realize the fact that his own generation of men was doomed to perish utterly. Greece, led by Alexander of Macedon, also had reigned far and wide. Alexander, according to legend, wept upon the banks of the Indus River to think that he had no more worlds to conquer. Now Greek strength, too, lay crumbled into bits. As for Carthage, the great African city blazed merrily. Scipio wept for his defeated enemy because he had the vision to foresee Rome's own ultimate doom.

As for Greece, that land was already finished as a Mediterranean power. Her role in history had passed from the positive to the negative role. However, this shift was not acknowledged publicly until the year 196 B.C., when a Roman proconsul named Flamininus made it official.

A Germanic medallion depicting a mounted warrior

In that year, at the Isthmian Games (athletic contests sponsored by Corinth), Flamininus arose to declare that henceforward Rome would act as the divinely appointed "Protector" of Greece. Some members of his audience sat stunned, while others cheered, and still more sighed with sad relief.

Half a century later, Greece took part in an ill-starred Asiatic revolt against Roman oppression. The response was crushing. To set a clear example to the rest of the country, as the Romans self-righteously explained, rich Corinth was leveled to the ground. Lucius Mummius, the Roman general in charge of that operation, took pains to have the sacred statuary of Corinth crated up for shipment to Rome. The shipments were insured, and Mummius insisted that if any works of art were lost in transit they should be replaced by others "just as good." The sensibilities of people in command seldom kept pace with their terrible power. It never occurred to Mummius that carvings by such gentle masters as Phidias and Praxiteles can never be replaced. He turned central Greece and the Peloponnesus into a minor dependency known as the Province of Achaea.

Greece served as a battleground for Julius Caesar and Pompey in

An early Christian adaptation of the crucifix combining Christ's monogram with an alpha and omega, symbolizing the beginning and end

Rome's first civil war, but that is no part of our story. Caesar's affair with Cleopatra has, however, some little pertinence. She was the last of the royal line founded at Alexandria by General Ptolemy. Brilliant as well as beautiful, and fully royal in spirit, she recalls Alexander's mother, Queen Olympias of Epirus. When Julius Caesar's assassination shattered Cleopatra's power base within the Roman government, she recouped by seducing his avenger, Mark Antony. A naval battle in Greek waters off Actium won the Roman Empire for a new Caesar, Augustus. He was too cold a man for Cleopatra ever to seduce. At age thirty-four, with Antony gone and possibly her own beauty fading, she killed herself. Augustus thereafter ruled that Roman officers should not so much as visit Alexandria without his own express permission. Egypt was too corrupting, the emperor explained.

Augustus was a hard and unappealing man, but he imposed the Peace of Rome from the Rhine and the Danube down to the Sahara, and from Britain all the way to Babylon. Then, at that rare moment of world calm, the Prince of Peace was born.

The common tongue of the eastern Mediterranean was Greek. Jesus spoke to His disciples in Aramaic, of course, but when He addressed Pontius Pilate and the like He, too, must have spoken in Greek. The four Apostles wrote their Gospels in Greek. One of their number, John, was evidently steeped in Greek philosophy. "In the beginning was the Word," he writes, and that assertion instantly reconciles Platonic thought to the experience of the Hebrew prophets.

In Jesus' time, the Jews of the Dispersion already numbered seven million, by some estimates. They spoke the tongues of the countries into which they were born, Greek being the commonest. The Jews of Alexandria preached the Old Testament—the Septuagint—in Greek. Hebrew synagogues stood scattered from one end of the classical world to the other, and they were hospitable. Many Gentiles found themselves drawn away from the proliferation of pagan cults and magical practices to the monotheism and moral rigor of the Jewish faith. Even without undergoing circumcision, these semiconverts were accepted by the Jews as "Fearers of the Lord."

All this helps explain the fact that Jesus' disciples and the Apostle Paul were able to spread the "good news" of Christ's incarnation, death, and subsequent resurrection so successfully. Within a scant three

decades they converted a significant portion of the common people of
the Roman Empire to Christianity. But there are still further reasons
back of this phenomenon which bear specifically upon the cultural history of Greece. For a long time before the coming of Jesus, it appears,
Greek thinkers and doers had helped prepare a bridge for Him.

Alexander the Great had been among the first of these. As Plutarch
later wrote, Alexander did not "treat the Greeks as if he were their
leader and the barbarians as if he were their master. He did not culti-
vate the Greeks as friends and relations while behaving to the barbarians as if they were animals or plants. He believed that he had a mission
from God to bring men into harmony with each other and to reconcile
the world." This seems extravagant praise, perhaps, for a man of
the sword. But Plutarch expressed the opinion most commonly held
concerning Alexander's deepest motivation. When the Conqueror
emerged from his tent and cried out to his troops, "But you are all my
kinsmen!" he meant it. His army, which responded to the cry with an
immediate hymn of victory, believed Alexander's implied assertion of
the brotherhood of man.

Among philosophers, Socrates in particular helped prepare the way
for Christianity. To many Greeks, his martyrdom appeared in retro-
spect as a foreshadowing of Jesus' own.

Socratic simplicity of life style was adopted by many of his followers, none more extreme perhaps than the "cynic" Diogenes. Cynic
means "dog-like" in Greek. Diogenes earned this epithet by living like
a stray dog on the streets. Alexander himself once met Diogenes and
asked what he could do for him. "You're standing in my sunlight," the
sage replied. "Move over." The Conqueror, retreating, told his friends
that if he were not himself he would like to be Diogenes. Rough though
he was in manner and conversation alike, Diogenes also stood for the
brotherhood of man. Asked where he hailed from, he replied, "I am a
cosmopolitan." He meant the same thing as the American philosopher
of revolution, Tom Paine, who said, "the world is my country."

The founder of the Stoic school at Athens, whose name was Zeno,
worked out the logical conclusions of such sentiments. He held, according to Plutarch, "that we should regard all men as fellow-parish-
ioners and fellow-citizens. There ought to be one way of life and one
system of order, as it were of one flock on a common pasture feeding

all together under a common law." The relevance of this pre-Christian doctrine to the teachings of Jesus and His disciples is obvious. In the brotherhood of Christ, as Saint Paul put the case, was "neither Greek nor Jew . . . Barbarian, Scythian, bond, nor free." Final union of the children of God would obliterate all such dichotomies, including the most grievous split of all, which was between slaves and free people. Slavery was of course the worst great curse of the classical world. Here is the place to look at it in more detail, since slaves made particularly strong recruits to Christianity.

Socrates was once offered a gift of slaves from a rich friend. He refused them. Virtue, Socrates understood, was no class privilege. "Stop to think," he cautioned his friends, "whether it is your slave or yourself who deserves a whipping." Moreover, he once coaxed a geometrical theorem from an illiterate slave boy in order to prove that wisdom is inborn in everyone.

Plato was less clear, perhaps, on that difficult point. His chief political dialogues, the *Republic* and the *Laws*, are rigidly authoritarian. In the ideal state envisioned by him, only philosophers were free. He thought that those philosophers would be members of the Establishment. The sad fact is that Socrates, who championed free critical inquiry, would hardly have survived a day in Plato's heavenly city. Yet at the same time Plato does seem to have possessed some dim vision of what Jesus was to mean when He said: "Consider the lilies of the field. . . ." God alone, Plato wrote, "is worthy of supreme seriousness. But man is God's plaything, and that is the best part of him. Therefore every man and woman should live life accordingly, and play the noblest games, and be of another mind from what they are at present. For example, people ought not to take war seriously. In war there is neither play nor education worthy of the name."

Rather ruefully, in his turn, Aristotle noted that the leisure required to make room for play and for education depended upon the institution of slavery. He himself kept slaves, although Aristotle set an important precedent by freeing them in his will. He was a pioneer of science, but naturally Aristotle never guessed that science itself would one day render human slavery obsolete.

We tend to picture the slaves of the classical world as having been worked to death under the lash. That did happen, of course. The condi-

An early Christian ivory represents Mary and other mourners at Christ's sepulcher, while He is shown, above, ascending into Heaven.

tions of slave labor in the Athenian silver mines near Sounion—to offer a single example—were notorious. As a rule, however, efficiency and economy demanded that slaves be rather carefully treated. House slaves did more than fetch and carry; they often served as governesses and tutors to the children. They, in particular, therefore, were fitted both to learn and to teach the new Christian dispensation. So, too, were the "organization men" of the Greek and Roman mercantile economy. The middle and lower echelons of business in the time of Christ were very largely filled by slaves. It should be noticed in passing that the biggest business of all was slavery itself. The sacred island of Delos had been transformed into an entrepôt for the eastern Mediterranean slave market. At peak seasons on that tiny and lovely island, ten thousand human beings were bought and sold every day. The Greco-Roman villas with their beautiful mosaic floors which may still be seen at Delos belonged to slave merchants.

"As I would not wish to be a slave, I would not wish to be a master either." That was the position of the Stoics, according to Diogenes Laertius. With Zeno and his followers, Greek philosophy arrived at the same views which were to be expressed in the distant future by Abraham Lincoln. So thoughtful slaveowners, too, were now prepared in their own minds for the revolutionary message of Jesus.

What about woman's position? It was hardly superior to that of slaves. Even glorious Pericles, who owed so much to his lady Aspasia, advised the women of Athens that they should keep and cherish personal obscurity. A Hellenistic treatise written at Alexandria and called *The Questions of Ptolemy* warned: "Remember, O King, that womankind is headstrong, hot in the pursuit of its own wishes, apt to change readily for want of sound reasoning, and naturally weak. For these reasons, women should be prudently handled. One had best not quarrel with them."

So much for the supercilious Greek view. Jewish men, unhappily, went so far as to thank God in their prayers that they had not been born female. Yet Judaism seems to have been particularly appealing to Gentile women. Josephus, the ancient Jewish historian, reported, "Many Greeks have come over to our Laws." The women of Damascus, he added, were "addicted to the Jewish religion." Nero's empress, Poppaea, was said to be a secret sympathizer with the Jews. These conver-

The apostles Peter and Paul, portrayed in a stone bas-relief

sions probably occurred because, for all the flat paternalism of their faith, the Jews possessed a deep sense of social justice—which women in particular could appreciate. This was to be the case with Christianity as well. Moreover, women especially understood the tender relation of Jesus to the three Marys. For them to welcome the new dispensation was only natural.

When active and worldly force falls to dust, the invisible power of passive transformation may reach its apogee. So it was with Greece in the time of Christ. Greece had nurtured a very profound, far-reaching pagan faith which centered upon Delphi. Again, Greece had given birth to Western philosophy, and with it the hope of discovering truth. Faith and Hope, then, were hers. Charity, or love, Greece had not yet achieved. That comes by inspiration, from without, and the Apostle Paul was the man who brought it to Greece. The story of how he did so is told in the *Acts of the Apostles,* which Luke, his companion, wrote. Saint Luke himself appears to have been Greek. Luke's account of their adventures gives a vivid picture of everyday Greek life. It describes

extremely modest events and victories. Yet Paul's experiences as a preacher were to prove even more momentous in the long run than the exploits of Alexander the Great.

Paul was a Hellenized Jew, a native of Asia Minor, and honorary citizen of Rome. His mission on behalf of Christ brought him and Luke to the site of ancient Troy, where Achilles, Xerxes, and Alexander had once sacrificed to pagan gods and sworn to do great deeds. As for Paul, he lay down, simply, and dreamed a dream. It seemed to him that a Macedonian spearman stood over his bed, saying: "Come across into Macedonia and help us." That was all there was to it. "When Paul had this vision," Saint Luke reports, "we immediately made ready to go to Macedon, since God had called us to preach the Gospel there."

They settled in the town of Philippi, which had no synagogue. Paul used to preach on the riverbank outside the city gate. He was much annoyed by a slave girl who kept crying, "These men can tell you how to save your souls!" Paul learned that the girl was gifted with second sight, and that her owners had become rich by hiring out her services as a fortuneteller. Doubtless this circumstance angered him yet further. Turning to face the wild-eyed girl, he commanded the spirit of prophecy to go away and leave her in peace. Instantly, the girl was calm. As she no longer prophesied, her owners accused Paul of destroying their source of income. The Apostle was hustled off to jail, flogged, and left with his feet clamped in stocks. Some other prisoners were in the cell with him. Paul preached, and prayed, and sang hymns. At midnight, the jail suddenly shook. The prisoners' fetters fell from the walls. The doors flew open. The jailer, in his guardroom, drew a sword to kill himself. He preferred that fate to the slow death which would be his punishment for letting the prisoners escape. Paul, however, glimpsed the jailer's action through the door. He shouted at once: "Don't harm yourself! We are all here." The jailer called for lights, entered Paul's cell, fell on his knees, and asked, "What must I do in order to be saved?" So Paul had a new convert to show for his own brief suffering and the midnight act of God. In the morning he was released with suitable apologies. The magistrates would not have had Paul flogged, they said, if they had known he was a citizen of Rome.

Moving on through Amphipolis, Apollonia, and Thessalonike, Paul reached Athens. The ancient town was shrunken inside of its volumi-

This sixth-century icon illustrating scenes from the gospel was originally the lid of a Byzantine reliquary.

nous walls. There was still a great deal of sacred statuary, however. The beauty of those things, Paul could not see. He went down to the market place and began preaching against idolatry. As a result, he was summoned before the Areopagus, Athens' oldest court, to answer the charge of propagating outlandish deities. This was not considered too grave an offense because, as Luke explains, "Athenians liked nothing so much as gossiping about the latest novelty." Paul used the occasion to deliver a sermon. Socrates, long before him, had done much the same thing. But times were easier now that Athens had become a half-ruined backwater. Nothing seemed to matter so much any more. Smiling and yawning behind their hands, the council members listened tolerantly as Paul proclaimed: "I have perambulated Athens and the Acropolis to gaze upon your objects of worship. Among the altars I have seen was one which bore an inscription saying, *To the Unknown God.* That deity, which you worship in ignorance, I can make known to you." Paul went on to speak of Christ's resurrection from the dead. At that point, he was interrupted by general laughter. The council dismissed him, without a reprimand.

It is much easier to convert a sinner than a theologian. Teachers, often enough, are the last to be taught. It may have been for these reasons that Paul soon abandoned Athens for Corinth, where he settled down. Corinth had risen from its ashes to become a notorious port of call for pleasure seekers and a sailors' town. Its temple of Aphrodite boasted a thousand priestess-prostitutes of renowned charms.

Like every mercantile center on the Mediterranean, Corinth also had its Jewish community. The Jews of Corinth were hospitable to Paul at first, but his teaching shocked most of them. Barred from the synagogue, he swore: "Let this be on your heads. I shall preach to the Gentiles, in any case." In a dream, Jesus comforted him and promised that he would come to no harm from the people of Corinth. So Paul stayed on for eighteen months. While at Corinth, he managed to set up the nucleus of a Christian community. That done, he set sail for Ionia. His missionary journeys were to carry him to Jerusalem and westward again all the way to Rome.

Paul's first letter back to the Christian community at Corinth bears quoting at length. This epistle stands with the purest lines of Homer, and with Plato's profoundest thoughts, in historic significance. The key

word of Paul's letter is *agape*—Greek for "love." The word became *caritas* in Latin. King James' translators of the Latin Bible rendered *caritas* in turn as "charity." Yet "love" appears the more appropriate word. With that substituted, the King James' text would read:

"Though I speak with the tongues of men and of angels, and have not love, I am become as a sounding brass, or a tinkling cymbal.

"And though I have the gift of prophecy, and understand all mysteries, and all knowledge; and though I have all faith, so that I could remove mountains, and have not love, I am nothing.

"And though I bestow all my goods to feed the poor, and though I give my body to be burned, and have not love, it profiteth me nothing.

"Love suffereth long, and is kind; love envieth not; love vaunteth not itself, is not puffed up.

"Doth not behave itself unseemly, seeketh not her own, is not easily provoked, thinketh no evil;

"Rejoiceth not in iniquity, but rejoiceth in the truth; Beareth all things, believeth all things, hopeth all things, endureth all things.

"Love never faileth; but whether there be prophecies, they shall fail; whether there be tongues, they shall cease; whether there be knowledge, it shall vanish away.

"For we know in part, and we prophesy in part.

"But when that which is perfect is come, then that which is in part shall be done away.

"When I was a child, I spake as a child, I understood as a child, I thought as a child: but when I became a man, I put away childish things.

"For now we see through a glass, darkly; but then face to face; now I know in part; but then shall I know even as also I am known.

"And now abideth faith, hope, love, these three; but the greatest of these is love."

About the year 67 A.D., Paul met his martyrdom on the Appian Way outside Rome. In deference to his Roman citizenship he was not crucified, but beheaded. Saint Peter was crucified head-down, nearby, on the same day. Rome had struck a shrewd double blow against revolutionary religion. But it was too late, as we know. The Greeks and Jews together had already built a bridge into eternity and back again, a bridge which no temporal power ever could destroy.

CHAPTER VII

BYZANTIUM
THE
SPLENDID

Reduced at last to the position of a relatively unimportant province of Rome, Greece remained significant on a different plane. Greece lived largely as a language and a culture from the time of the Roman take-over until the nineteenth century. As a political entity, she slept for more than two thousand years. Yet her dreams, so to speak, were an illumination of Europe and the world during that entire period. The best minds of the early Church Fathers and of the Roman emperors alike were all attuned to Hellenic philosophy. As Clement of Alexandria put the case: "Philosophy was necessary to the Greeks for righteousness."

Clement's follower, Origen, noted that certain Greek philosophers recognized the word of God as the ordering principle of the cosmos. "In this," Origen commented, "they write what is agreeable not only to the law but to the Gospel as well. Moral and, as it is called, physical philosophy take the same view as we do at most points."

From the early Christian perspective upon history it seemed that Socrates had been a prophet crying in a marble wilderness. Alexander the Great also had foreshadowed what was to come when he attempted

A bronze bust of Constantine, founder of the Eastern Orthodox empire

to impose a peace upon all nations. As Socrates rehearsed the mystery of the martyrdom of God, so Alexander rehearsed for a brief moment of historic time the Pax Romana which Caesar Augustus would impose.

"Augustus," Origen remarks, "leveled together under his one kingship the many inhabitants of the earth. Now it would have been a hindrance to the spread of the teaching of Jesus through all the world if there had been many kingdoms." This line of reasoning led the early Christians to wholehearted acceptance of a one-world political concept. They were only too happy to follow the express command of Christ to "Render unto Caesar the things that are Caesar's and to God the things that are God's." But an insurmountable problem arose when, for reasons of political expediency, the Roman emperors themselves insisted (just as Alexander the Great had done) upon being recognized as divine. Christians could not acquiesce in paying such homage. To them it appeared blasphemous.

In a passage pregnant with significance and tragedy, Origen pointed out that "there are two types of law set before us. One is the law of Nature which is such as God would enact. The other is the written law of cities. Where the written law is not opposed to the law of God, it is good that citizens should not forsake it on the plea that it is foreign to them. But where the law of Nature and of God ordains what is opposed to the written law, then consult your conscience. It may be that the innermost Word will tell you to bid farewell to what is written and to the will of the lawgivers. Then give yourself to God and choose to live according to His Word even at the price of being scorned and subjected to every conceivable danger and tribulation."

Christians who were thrown to the lions in the Colosseum at Rome obeyed the principles which Origen expressed. So have a great many more persons of conscience, Christian and otherwise, down to the present day. Recent examples are sure to spring to almost every reader's mind. It may be noted here that among the Founding Fathers of the United States was one who made a profound study of Origen; namely Thomas Jefferson.

For some three centuries and more after the crucifixion and resurrection of the Christ, the Mediterranean world remained officially pagan. The Roman emperor Hadrian considered Athens his spiritual home, and he was initiated into the still-flourishing mysteries of Eleusis.

Hadrian built a library for the Athenian public. Near the library he
erected a clock tower with sundials and bas-reliefs depicting the winds
ornamenting its eight outside walls. "The Tower of the Winds," as it
is called, still stands in the midst of Athens. Its original clock was an
Alexandrian device, a sort of flagpole socketed down into a tube of
water. The water escaped drop by drop, and as its level sank the pole
subsided minute by minute. The teachings of the great Athenian Stoics
were not lost upon Hadrian, nor, for that matter, upon any cultivated
Roman. Stoicism's moral tone appealed to them. So did the milder in-
junctions of a rival Athenian school, the Epicureans, who counseled
cultivating one's own garden.

The *Meditations* of the emperor Marcus Aurelius synthesize those
two late streams of Stoicism and Epicureanism. Marcus Aurelius wrote
in Greek, although his notes were certainly addressed to his own heart.
A brief quotation from them will suffice to show how advanced pagan
thought paralleled Christian concepts. "A man lives with the gods,"
the pious emperor wrote, "if he always presents to their view a soul
that is satisfied with what they give; a soul which does the will of the
daemon sent by Zeus as a particle of His own Being, to be his protector
and governor."

Plotinus of Alexandria was the last of the great philosophers descended from Plato and the pagan mysteries. His *Enneads*, written
about the middle of the third century A.D., owe nothing overt to Christianity. Yet Christian mystics ever since have claimed Plotinus as a
father of a kind. Plotinus links classical culture to modern Christian
aspiration. There is no room to quote more than a fragment of his
work, but something at least must be given. Everyone has read a little
Plato, yet Plotinus is relatively unknown. Here is a typical passage:

"But what must we do? How lies the path? How come to vision the
inaccessible Beauty, dwelling as if in consecrated precincts, apart from
the common ways where all men may see? Let us flee to the beloved
Fatherland. This is the soundest counsel. But what is the flight? How
are we to gain the open sea? The Fatherland is There whence we have
come, and There is the Father."

The noble simplicity of a Saint Paul, or Origen, or Marcus Aurelius,
or Plotinus, is their common denominator after all. Each of those men
appeared to gaze inward upon a single source of his own being, with

OVERLEAF: *Ninth-century battle between Byzantine and Arab cavalrymen, as depicted in the later chronicle of John Scylitzes*

εβρεῖας καὶ τῶν γαρέκ πῶσων ἐρσων· καὶ ἀφ
ἀμειοσρόιο· ἐμεωπιπεῖτοιο κατὰ μετω πωσον
πληγειο· αὐτοσ τε πιπει· καὶ τοῦ μεαυτοῦ

υπαθεου
σολιτου

ομερος δε τὴν ἠ τ πανο τούτου ἰησ ελο προ μομι
μηρα ιωπεδιδρασκερ· ἀλλα καὶ τοῦ του το το

ακαπερονοσερειραιτασορ | αυτον : τοτεδ[υ]
ορμεταοφοδραστωροσβολησ · ἔνπακα[
ωξεπαιουδεειο

οιτουανμὸ

αμφοιωαποσφαλειοτουσρατου · ἀθύτωροσ
εσιαυουκλεισουραρχηνκαπαδιωξαο · χε

full attention. Sadly, that way of thinking barely survived the ultimate triumph of Christianity in the political sphere.

Emperor Constantine the Great was Christianity's crucial convert, from a worldly viewpoint. When he came to the throne, possibly one in ten of his subjects was a Christian. His Edict of Milan, granting Christians religious freedom, gave them legal defense against further persecution. But that was only the beginning. By the time of Constantine's death in the year 337, the Christian Church had already become an instrument of persecution in its turn. The Council of Nicaea (325), presided over by the emperor himself, had laid down rules of belief to which all bishops and their flocks were thereafter expected to adhere. Christians who consulted their own consciences, as suggested by Origen, might now find themselves engaged in life-and-death conflict with their own authorities. In fact, the world soon began ringing with "heresies" and the groans of people meaninglessly martyred in ecclesiastical civil wars. The disputes hinged upon what would now be called semantic distinctions. For example, an Alexandrian archbishop named Arius argued that since Christ was the son of God He must be younger than the Father and not precisely consubstantial with Him. The Council of Nicaea stamped that as heretical. Again, certain theologians were consigned to eternal hell-fire for daring to maintain that since Christ was the son of God and Mary He must have had two distinct natures in Himself. Others were equally condemned for opposite assertions. Monophysites held that the divine in Christ entirely absorbed the human element. The orthodox position, which prevailed in general, amounted to an elaborate and paradoxical patterning of abstractions. According to triumphant authority, Christ did indeed exhibit a double nature which was at one and the same time unmixed, unchangeable, indistinguishable, and inseparable.

The people caught up in such metaphysical struggles might lose their lives—and be threatened with eternal damnation in the bargain— for the sake of an ambiguous syllable or two. Not only that, but cities and even nations suffered destruction in the all-holy but infinitely debatable name of God.

Not even Constantine the Great could overcome these nightmare difficulties or succeed in setting the first great Christian nation on a truly Christian path of forgiveness and toleration. Yet Constantine did

accomplish miracles. From his day to the present moment, Greeks have revered Constantine as the true founding father of the Orthodox Greek world. He has often been called "the thirteenth Apostle."

On the site of the Greek city of Byzantium, on the western shore of the Bosporus which divides Europe's southeastern corner from Asia, Constantine built a new capital in 330. The Roman imperial city took his own name, as Constantinople. It was to be the chief hub and fortress of human aspiration until it fell to the Ottoman Turks in 1453, eleven hundred and twenty-three years later. Gradually, it ceased to be Roman. Constantinople became Eastern in opulence, Greek in language, Hebrew in fanaticism, Alexandrian in scholarship, and Christian in religion. In short, it was far more of a cosmopolis than Rome had been.

All through the Dark Ages of Europe, until the beginnings of the Renaissance, Byzantium, as the empire came to be called, flourished with a splendor which perhaps has never been equaled by any earthly power before or since. The walls of Constantinople were barrier reefs against barbarian tidal waves coming from all directions. The city itself often stood in danger and yet it proved more long-lived and stable than Rome had been. The Balkan peoples and the Russians, who received their alphabet and their religion alike from Byzantine missionaries, give due importance in their history books, their legends, and their prayers, to the soldiers and saints of ancient Byzantium. As for the Greeks, they still see ancient Constantinople as their spiritual home.

The creative side of Byzantine culture is coming to be appreciated everywhere. The careful codification of laws and legal precedents was not a Roman invention so much as it was Byzantine. The literary men of Constantinople were mainly commentators and compilers, it is true, but they put together the invaluable *Greek Anthology* of classical poetry, along with curious works on court usage and etiquette. The erudite and gossipy historians Procopius and Psellus wrote chronicles of their own times which possess undying interest.

The new artists of Byzantium turned their backs upon three-dimensional monument making in the Hellenistic mode. Rather, their glittering visions were recorded in the medium of mosaics, made by setting bits of glass close together in wet plaster to cover vast wall spaces. Their works may still be seen in fragments here and there, although at least 99 per cent of what they did has been destroyed in various wars

or plastered over by conquering Moslems. The best examples still extant are at the Church of Chora in Istanbul, at Ravenna and Messina in Italy, and at Daphne near Athens. Byzantine artists also practiced fresco painting, which was to achieve new brilliance with Giotto and the Italian Renaissance. More typical, however, were their pictures dealing with sacred subjects and painted on small portable wooden panels. These "icons"—Greek for "images"—may be found together with more recent works of the same kind in every Greek Orthodox church. Manuscript illumination, enameling, and miniature carving in ivory were Byzantine specialties also. Embroideries of silk with gold and silver thread were manufactured at Constantinople. It was a Byzantine emperor named Justinian who first imported silkworms from China. To him also belongs the credit for having built the church of Sancta Sophia—"Holy Wisdom."

Sancta Sophia, or Hagia Sophia as it is alternately known, was transformed into a mosque at the time of the Turkish conquest. It still stands, and to enter it is every bit as awesome an experience as climbing to the ruins of the Parthenon. With the construction of this church, a seminal new architectural principle was introduced. Namely, the superimposition of a dome upon a square with pendentives at the corners to bind the two shapes into one. That seems a small advance, perhaps, but it comforts the soul of man by recapitulating in architectural language the relation of earth to heaven. None of Sancta Sophia's descendants really compare with this great edifice, but they include the Capitol at Washington and Saint Peter's Basilica at Rome.

In order to get some idea of courtly ceremonial at Constantinople, witness a high mass in a great cathedral. The priests' vestments are very like what Byzantine courtiers were wont to wear, and the traditional bishops' attire echoes that of the ancient emperors. The prostrations, elevations, and liturgical choruses reflect on a sacerdotal plane the secular splendors of Byzantium. The organ music which we tend to associate with church was long scorned in Europe as a product of Byzantine sensuality. An Alexandrian Greek scientist invented the organ. Byzantine emperors used to present the instrument to barbarian potentates as gifts, on occasion.

There was, incidentally, an extremely influential and secret "Barbarian Office" at Constantinople. Like the secret intelligence agencies

This manuscript illumination shows Byzantine Emperor John VI settling a theological dispute at a council of patriarchs in 1351.

employed by the great powers of the present day, that Office maneuvered to promote the empire's interests at the expense of the rest of the world. The epithet "Byzantine diplomacy" is still used to imply double-dealing, wholesale bribery, and the fomenting of discord abroad. That sort of thing saved Constantinople on many occasions. When it failed, the city still had its immense fortifications to fall back upon and wealth enough to attract entire armies of mercenary troops. The emperor's own Varangian Guard, to give just one example, was made up of horn-helmeted Norsemen from as far away as Iceland. They used to be paid off in pure gold.

Constantinople's seemingly bottomless wealth came from two sources in particular. The first was the manufacturing of luxury items and the creation of portable works of art within the city's walls. These things, produced under an elaborately regulated guild system, were everywhere in demand. Trade, however, brought in still greater revenue. For century after century, the Golden Horn, as Constantinople's port was known, controlled the major flow of trade shipments among three continents. The city's commercial connections extended from China to Great Britain and from the Baltic to the Red Sea. All this did not by any means eliminate poverty within the empire. Taxes were high, and the peasantry hard pressed. The city itself, however, could boast what amounted to socialized medicine and free education at university level.

The chariot races at the hippodrome used to generate tremendous excitement city-wide. Rioting and even revolutions sprang from the popular passion for the sport. Religious disputes were exacerbated by conflicting loyalties to various chariot teams. Crushing police action followed by incredibly magnificent pageantry would restore the city's calm. An empress might be displayed riding in solemn procession to a ritual immersion, surrounded by maidens tossing pearl-encrusted apples in their hands. Or the True Cross—discovered by Constantine's mother—might be brought out to perambulate the city in its glittering sheath of gems.

Space is too short for this subject. The atmosphere of Constantinople can hardly be conveyed in a few brief flashes. But on the other hand, no history of Greece would be complete without a summary, at least, of Byzantium's fortunes. If the Greek center of gravity moved

from Athens to Alexandria in Hellenistic times, it shifted northeast-ward to the Bosporus on the day that Constantine founded his capital.

Constantine's immediate successors were chiefly occupied with ward-ing off Persian and Germanic incursions. Fortunately, they found them-selves well placed from the military point of view. The city controlled the passage to the Black Sea more effectively than Troy had ever done. It drew Greek-speaking and battle-loving recruits from Asia Minor, Thrace, Macedonia, and Greece itself. Its sea walls and massive land walls were proof against the siege techniques, battering rams, and cata-pults of the ancient world. Yet almost from the very beginnings of Byzantium, the empire had insistent dangers to overcome. One of the first was internal, brought about by the apostasy of the emperor Julian.

Educated at Athens, and cosmopolitan in the philosophical sense of the term, Julian did his best to break the growing symbiosis be-tween Church and empire. He called for toleration, at least, of non-Christian faiths. As for himself, he said, he would be a pagan of the old school. Julian sent an ambassador to Delphi asking what the fate of his plans would be.

"Tell the King," the message came, "that the fair hall has fallen to the ground. No longer has Phoebus Apollo a hut, nor a prophetic laurel, nor a spring that speaks. The water of speech even is quenched." Not long after that, in the year 363, Julian died on a campaign against Persia. He may well have been assassinated by a Christian soldier. Clas-sical paganism had breathed its last, at least in places of authority. From now on the Church was to be, for good or ill, Byzantium's heart and soul.

Theodosius the Great, fervently Orthodox, called an Ecumenical Council at Constantinople in the year 381. Its edicts forced a temporary agreement among the faithful all the way from York in Great Britain to the Euphrates River. After Theodosius' death, successive onslaughts of Visigoths, Huns, and Ostrogoths crumpled the western portion of the empire. Toward the middle of the fifth century yet another bar-barian tribe, the Vandals, successfully challenged Constantinople at sea and temporarily detached North Africa from the empire. The By-zantine response to such reverses was subtle and pacific more often than not. Missionary priests and smooth ambassadors laden with pre-cious gifts would be employed to convert key chieftains to Christianity.

HICDEFERTVRC ORPVSSCIMARCI

Whole hordes of barbarians would be welcomed to depopulated regions and enlisted under the emperor's nominal command.

Rome itself was soon given over to ferocious and fur-clad tribal leaders such as Stilicho and Alaric, who styled themselves the emperor's western lieutenants.

The archbishops of Rome, Alexandria, Antioch, and Constantinople quarreled continually over questions of faith and precedence. Rome, being the See of Peter, had claim to primacy. Constantinople, as the seat of power, was not about to bow to the shepherd of a ragged and semi-barbarous outpost. The quarrels which ensued would eventually culminate in tragedy for the entire Christian world.

At Constantinople, meanwhile, theological ferment bubbled merrily. As a contemporary clergyman, Gregory of Nyssa, ruefully noted: "The whole city is full of it, the squares, the market places, the crossroads, the alleyways; old clothes men, money-changers, food-sellers: they are all busy arguing. If you ask someone to give you change, he philosophizes about the Begotten and the Unbegotten; if you enquire about the price of a loaf, you are told by way of reply that the Father is greater and the Son inferior; if you ask 'Is my bath ready?' the attendant answers that the Son was made out of Nothing."

Justinian, of Macedonian peasant stock, dominated the Mediterranean world in the sixth century. Besides building Sancta Sophia and setting his whole administration on a plane of splendor such as the world had never seen, Justinian reconquered vast regions from the barbarians. His activities put such a strain upon the imperial treasury, however, as to weaken Byzantium in the long run. Justinian's supple-minded bride, the empress Theodora, was a former actress and courtesan with Asiatic connections. She led the emperor into the shoal waters of religious politics and apparently persuaded him to humiliate the See of Rome. His efforts to accommodate the Monophysite heresies popular at Antioch and Alexandria were rebuffed. Justinian's Fifth Ecumenical Council, held in 553, was a personal failure. Church historians still condemn Justinian's unremitting and authoritarian efforts to resolve the bishops' quarrels as "Caesaropapism." Worse yet, the majority of his subjects agreed that the emperor himself eventually succumbed to heresy.

The next century witnessed the spectacular triumphs and defeats of

A jeweled and enameled panel from a huge golden altar screen removed from Constantinople by Venetians and placed in Saint Mark's Cathedral

the emperor Heraclius. Many a war has been designated a "crusade," but Heraclius' campaign against Persia really deserves that name. When it began, the Persian kingdom of the Sassanids allied with the wild Avar tribes of the Eurasian steppe had engulfed the whole Near East and almost captured Constantinople as well. The Eastern allies also seized Christendom's most revered relic, the True Cross, from Jerusalem's Church of the Holy Sepulcher. This they carried off to the Persian capital. Heraclius had been a strangely inactive emperor until the precious relic was lost. Now he went right after it, with energy and courage reminiscent of Alexander the Great. And in 628, he crushed the Sassanids forever. Heraclius returned to Constantinople bearing the True Cross, with infinite pomp and ceremony, in his victory procession.

Legend relates that among the hundreds of ambassadors who congratulated him upon his victory there was one who had been sent by an Arabian sheik named Mohammed. This turbaned emissary suggested that the emperor might do well to adopt a new religion called Islam, Arabic for "peace." Heraclius is said to have smiled rather abstractedly, in his own joy, and dismissed the Bedouin with a generous present. So rapid was the rise of this totally unexpected menace that within the very next decade Islam burst from its desert bounds to vanquish a huge army under Heraclius in Palestine. The Mohammedans went on to capture Jerusalem and Alexandria.

The death of Heraclius saw Byzantium reduced to a largely Greek-speaking entity consisting of Asia Minor, Greece, the Balkan coastline, Sicily, and North Africa. The Holy See of Rome was now Lombard territory. The great bishoprics of Syria, Palestine, and Egypt had been shorn away by the Saracens.

In the eighth century, Leo the Isaurian set Byzantium once again upon a firm footing. He preserved the capital through a two-year Saracen siege and then sallied forth to beat the enemy back to the Armenian frontier. Leo saw his son Constantine V married to a princess of the wild Khazar people who controlled the region north of the Caspian Sea. Father and son alike were persons of fanatical force and single-mindedness, Mohammedan in temperament though Christian in religion. Brilliant rulers both, they have been made villains in Church history because of their "iconoclastic" policies. They ordered the suppression of all icons and other sacred images in churches throughout

the empire. Their edicts on this score accorded with both Hebrew and
Moslem practice, but were a source of deep offense to the West. The
pope at Rome, hard pressed as he was in any case, now cast the lot of
the Western Church with a Frankish champion, Charlemagne.

As the first Holy Roman Emperor, Charlemagne dreamed of unit-
ing all Christendom once again by marrying the first female emperor
(not empress) of Byzantium. She was an Athenian-born woman named
Irene, who had come to the throne by deliberately blinding and thus
disqualifying the legitimate emperor. He happened to be her own son.
This wickedness on Irene's part was pretty much the usual thing in
court circles in Constantinople. Out of a hundred and nine Byzantine
sovereigns, three were starved to death, twelve perished in prison,
eighteen were blinded or castrated, and sixty-five assassinated. Byzantine government has been described as "absolute monarchy tempered
by assassination." The wonder is that the institution survived all that
internal bloodshed. What kept it going surely, was the popular faith
that whoever managed to seize the throne had God on his side.

As a Greek, the emperor Irene loved images. She had "iconoclasm"
branded as heresy, and brought back icons into Byzantine churches
again. Irene might well have accepted Charlemagne's offer of marriage
in the year 802 had she not herself been overthrown by a usurper. He
was her finance minister, who became Nicephorus I.

Nicephorus was slain in battle against a new menace: the Bulgars.
For the next century or so, Byzantium stood in danger of being crushed
between two millstones: Bulgars and Saracens.

In the year 1014, the emperor Basil "Bulgaroctonus" (Bulgar-
slayer) destroyed the Bulgar power. He took 15,000 prisoners in a
single battle, and blinded nearly all of them. Basil left one eye to one
prisoner in each hundred, and assigned that man to lead his companions
home. Their king died of apoplexy when he saw them. That eliminated
a major threat, but minor incursions and brush-fire rebellions kept
things interesting in a military sense. In 1040, to give just one example
out of hundreds, the Christianized Slavic population of Athens rose
against the emperor's tax gatherers. Athens was brought under control
again by a detachment of the imperial Varangian Guard commanded
by a huge Norseman named Harald Haardraade. He was to be slain
in William the Conqueror's 1066 invasion of Britain.

By the end of the eleventh century, Normans threatened Byzantium. The emperor Alexius I stopped their advance from Sicily at a high price. He made an alliance with Venice, the rising sea power. Venetian traders were allotted a section of Constantinople itself, together with commercial rights which would slowly bleed white the Byzantine economy. Alexius also welcomed the First Crusade of Frankish forces into Asia, and viewed with satisfaction its successes against his hereditary enemies, the Seljuk Turks.

In the year 1204, the Venetians diverted a crusade originally aimed at the Holy Land and hurled it against Constantinople. The walls were breached and the city thoroughly sacked. In Sancta Sophia, a Parisian prostitute seated herself on the patriarch's throne while knights drank from the altar vessels, trampled icons underfoot, and ripped down the silken wall hangings to make wrappings for their loot. The rape and pillaging went on for three days. During that time a large part of the creative work of a millennium was undone. Never before or since did a single city yield up so much treasure so suddenly. Nor has there been a greater crime committed against civilization than this one. The Fourth Crusade, so-called, will live in infamy.

The conquerors divided what had been Byzantium into feudal fiefs bearing such names as the "Empire of Romania," the "Kingdom of Salonika," the "Duchy of Athens," and the "Duchy of the Archipelago." All these acquisitions proved ephemeral, however. They were destroyed by internecine wars, the brutal indifference of Frankish overlords, popular unrest among the Greeks, and finally, an almost miraculous resurgence of Byzantine power. In the year 1261 a new Byzantine emperor named Michael Palaeologus recaptured Constantinople. As his troops surged into the city, the Frankish ruler Baldwin II, the Roman Catholic archbishop, and the Venetian podesta sailed away westward down the Hellespont.

What followed was a time of weakness combined with a surprising Indian summer of Byzantine culture. The revived empire could not last very long, obviously. The trade which had kept Byzantine finances more or less solvent through thick and thin was now entirely dominated by Venice and Genoa. Constantinople still led the world in the manufacture of luxury goods and the creation of artworks, but this only made the city a tempting prize. Moreover a new threat was rising in

the mountains of Anatolia. The Ottoman Turks would soon engulf Constantinople for good and all.

Yet in her extreme old age and well-justified fear of death, the city exhibited exquisite cultivation and *joie de vivre*. This can be seen in the art of the period, particularly the mosaics and frescoes at Chora Church. Semiautonomous outposts of Byzantium at Trebizond on the Black Sea and at Mistra near ancient Sparta also were filled with gallant spirit. The very beautiful art still to be seen in the churches of Mistra breathes an atmosphere of happy chivalry.

In the spring of 1453, the Ottoman conqueror Mohammed II laid Constantinople under siege. The Western world seemed utterly indifferent, despite the fact that Christendom as a whole owed its existence to the thousand years of shelter which Byzantium had provided. Some few Venetian and Genoese sailors, however, volunteered to defend the walls "for the honor of God and of all Christendom." It was too late for help. The walls were already crumbling under the drumfire of Sultan Mohammed's new weapon: cannonry. At the eleventh hour, a last solemn high mass was held in Sancta Sophia. Roman Catholic and Orthodox Greek buried their differences to take part as one in this brilliant rite. The next morning, the Turks burst in. For a second and final time, Constantinople was sacked. The Byzantine emperor, Constantine XI, is presumed to have perished in the rout. No one saw him fall. According to Greek legend, he will return.

Mohammed had a good deal of fighting still to do. He did not take Athens until 1456, nor Mistra until 1460. The next year he extinguished Byzantium's last glittering spark far to the east at Trebizond. Greek fortunes were never so low as at that moment, it appeared.

CHAPTER VIII

"I DREAMED THAT GREECE MIGHT STILL BE FREE"

Habitually, the Turks referred to their alien subjects as *rayah*. The word means "cattle." It was not a deliberate insult to the Greeks or any other subject people, but simply the expression of an attitude. The Turks had long been nomads, roaming the harsh Eurasian steppe and living in a precarious symbiotic relation to their flocks and herds. Now Constantinople, together with a steadily expanding empire, belonged to them. They were utterly dedicated to the spread of Islam. Their Christian subjects, naturally, felt no such dedication. Hence Christians within the Turkish orbit were regarded by their Ottoman masters as lacking true religion or nobility of spirit. That made them "cattle" from the Moslem viewpoint. Christians within the empire were forbidden to bear arms or to ride on horseback. Such activities would be unnatural for them, the Ottomans felt.

Every non-Moslem subject was compelled to pay a yearly "head tax" for the privilege of keeping his head on his shoulders. The alternative was decapitation. Every Christian family which produced as many as five male children was forced to deliver one son over to the Turks for education as a janissary. The word comes from the Turkish *yeniçeri*,

Adamantios Korais, theorist and educator at the time of the Greek Revolution

meaning "new troops." Janissaries formed an elite corps. (Moslem parents used to smuggle their children into Christian homes in the hope that they would be enrolled in the corps.) They were forbidden to marry. All their loyalty was at the sultan's command, and they were the keen edge of the sword of Islam. The only remotely comparable Christian soldiery were the Knights Templars and their various offshoots. This cruelest of all possible taxes at least assured a career for sons who were seized. By the same token, Christians could view the arbitrary culling of their most beautiful daughters with wistful complacency. Harem odalisques lived incarcerated in the utmost luxury, as a rule, and might even become the mothers of Ottoman pashas.

The prophet Mohammed had strictly enjoined his followers to allow religious freedom to "People of the Book." That included Jews, Christians, and the Zoroastrians of Persia, all of whom could point to written gospels of their own. Therefore the Greek Orthodox archbishop (or patriarch, as he was known) of Constantinople was carefully respected by the Ottomans.

With the exception of occasional levies of a son or daughter, Greeks of this time rendered unto the sultan the things that were the sultan's, and unto God the things that were God's. They were not compelled to bow down before false gods of empire, as their forefathers in Roman times had been, nor were they forced to go against the teachings of Jesus and "live by the sword." The subject Christians' lands were their own, at least in the sense that the pasturage belongs to the sheep. They were allowed to educate the children who were not taken away. This in itself assured the continuity of the Greek language and of Orthodox religion. Even the pagan gods of rural Greece returned in a new guise, as saints and angels ready to comfort the humble and the wise.

From the perspective of history, Greece had all but disappeared behind Turkey's damask curtain. Yet for the Greeks themselves life went on in a mood of unaccustomed quiet, peace, small joys, and domestic sorrows. It might not be too much to say that Turkish domination inadvertently helped Greeks practice what Christ had preached. They were forced to live as a mild and obedient flock, not unlike sheep—or "cattle," as the Ottomans said.

Mohammedan religious and secular law were one and the same. The Ottomans could not apply their legal system to infidels, so they put the

patriarch at Constantinople in control of Greek affairs generally. The patriarch became a kind of captive ruler for the captive half of Christendom. A Greek civil service gradually grew up around him. The subject bureaucrats were known as "Phanariots" after the "Phanar," or lighthouse quarter of Constantinople, which they inhabited. Their services insured the continuity of Greek civilization, even if in a semi-submerged state. On the other hand, the patriarch, the Phanariots, and the Orthodox clergy, all three of necessity supported Ottoman oppression. This was to result in much bitterness later on.

The Turks' most galling enemies, for some time, were the Venetians. Turkish cavalry thoroughly dominated the Balkans and the Greek mainland, but Venetian galleys ruled the sea. As Athens had done during the Peloponnesian War, Venice kept control of many Greek islands plus a few fortified coastal towns on the mainland.

Greeks who lived under the thumb of Venice were not permitted self-government. Moreover, they were forced to deny their Orthodox faith and bend the knee to Roman Catholic ritual and belief. This was no small thing from their viewpoint, since "heretical" practices appeared to lead in the direction of eternal damnation. So Venice got no help at all from the native population in her intermittent wars with the Turks. Those wars require no chronicling here. They achieved nothing of any permanence.

On the other hand, Venice was the main carrier of Greek culture to the West. That precious commerce must have seemed extremely incidental to the queenly city on the water. There was little money in it, and still less power. If history were written only in blood and in the flow of gold and silver coin, what the Greeks poured into Europe through Venice would be as nothing. But in fact their influence did much to shape the more positive aspects of Western civilization.

The story of that contribution goes back to 1438, when Gemistus Pletho of Mistra, and Cardinal Bessarion of Constantinople, landed at Venice in company with the great Western theologian Nicholas of Cusa. They were on their way to Florence, to attend an ecclesiastical congress. The congress failed to achieve its aim, which was to have been a last-minute reconciliation between the Eastern and Western Churches. But it opened Italian minds for the first time since the classical past to the direct illumination of Greek thought.

Pletho gave an epochal address in Florence called *On the Differences between Plato and Aristotle,* which helped break the strangle hold of certain half-understood Aristotelian concepts upon Western thought. As Marsilio Ficino wrote a generation afterward, it was Pletho who inspired the founding of Cosimo de' Medicis' Platonic Academy.

After Constantinople's final fall, Venice began receiving a steady flow of intellectuals and classicists from its own Greek possessions. One of the first was Michael Apostolis, who spent most of his life searching out and copying down Greek manuscripts on the island of Crete. He wrote an address with a very long title which begins, "Michael Apostolis to Those who Claim that the Westerners are Superior to the Easterners. . . ."

The peroration of that speech is graceful and passionate at the same time. "I say that you are the foremost," Apostolis confesses, "and that we are the remnants. Because, in the cycle of civilization which has a beginning, a middle, and an end, we are at the closing stage of our culture while you are in the initial phase. And we are enslaved whereas you are free."

Venice allotted a particular quarter of the city to Greek immigrants, and sponsored a chair for Greek studies at the University of Padua. Those things mattered. A Greek scholar of the early sixteenth century, Demetrius Ducas, sent a letter to a colleague which reads in part: "It is through your efforts, Musurus, in the celebrated and very renowned city of Padua, where you teach publicly from that Chair as from the height of a throne, that one sees depart each year from your school, as from the flanks of the Trojan horse, so many learned pupils that one could believe them born in the bosom of Greece or belonging to the race of the Athenians." (Among the students who came from all over Europe to study at Padua, by the way, were Copernicus, Vesalius, Galileo, and Harvey.)

In Venice itself, presses founded by Zacharias Callierghis and Aldus Manutius were making the Greek classics available to Europeans for the first time. Aldus found a powerful ally in the Northern humanist Desiderius Erasmus, whose work *In Praise of Folly* was the great best seller of the Renaissance. It revives the kindly and yet mocking, comic and yet austere, spirit of Socrates.

Not until the mid-sixteenth century and the long reign of Suleiman

The army of Sultan Murad III, carrying banners of Islam, celebrates victory in this miniature from a sixteenth-century Turkish manuscript.

the Magnificent did the Ottoman Empire reach its apogee. Suleiman defeated the Hungarian armies at Mohacs in the year 1526, but failed in his supreme effort to capture Vienna three years later. From then on, imperceptibly at first, Ottoman fortunes declined. Suleiman's successor, Selim the Sot, as he was rather unjustly known, captured Cyprus from Venice in 1571. Selim's navy suffered a terrible defeat in that same year. A Christian fleet recruited by the pope at Rome and under the command of Austria's Don Juan sank Turkish hopes of naval supremacy off Lepanto. Cervantes, author of the immortal *Don Quixote,* lost an arm in that battle. Thousands of Greek galley slaves, rowing under the whips of Christian and Moslem alike, were drowned.

Almost a hundred years later, in 1664, the Turks took a decisive beating on land from the Austrians at Saint Gotthard. Then Venice, itself in decline, overran the Peloponnesus and Attica. In the course of that particular campaign, Venetian artillery half destroyed the Athenian Parthenon. The Turks, under siege, were using the temple as a gunpowder magazine. A cannoneer in the Venetian forces lobbed a shell through the roof, and that was that.

The population of Greece and Anatolia alike was steadily decreasing. A British ambassador at Constantinople reported that one might ride through the countryside for six days at a stretch without coming upon a single village capable of feeding a man and his horse. The coastal towns and islands suffered periodic attack by Moslem and Christian corsairs from North Africa and from Catalonia and Italy. The mountain fastnesses of Greece were now controlled by Christian brigands known as "klephts," who preyed like wolves upon the valley farmers. In order to combat such threats as these, the Turks at last reversed their former policy and allowed subject Greeks to arm themselves. They also stopped seizing children for the janissary corps. Janissaries were now permitted to marry; and membership in the corps became hereditary. This privilege led to the slow diminution of military ardor followed by widespread corruption. Embattled as they were, the Ottomans more than once considered exterminating their remaining Greek subjects. Fortunately, they no longer possessed sufficient power to go that far. Besides, the captive infidels still constituted a major source of tax revenue. Accommodations were made accordingly. The Phanariots at Constantinople received increased power, and honor

as well. Greeks rose to high positions in the Sublime Porte (the Sultan's administration) itself. Two even became grand viziers. Turkish diplomacy and trade with the Western world were largely undertaken by Greek subjects.

The Ottomans themselves disdained commerce and found diplomatic negotiations somehow demeaning. Their ideals stemmed from the immemorial chivalric code of the Eurasian steppe. For a Mohammedan gentleman, to ride, to shoot straight, and to tell the truth were the important acquirements. The complexities of the new West both disgusted and baffled the Turks. So they let civic and commercial affairs slip into Greek hands. For example, the Ottomans appointed Greek subjects to be "Dragoman of the Porte" and "Dragoman of the Fleet," respectively. Those titles stood for "chief interpreter" in the Departments of State and Maritime Affairs, but in fact they carried full responsibility for both departments.

Phanariots meanwhile kept close connections with expatriate Greek merchant communities in London, Paris, Geneva, and Moscow—not to mention such ancient Greek ports of call as Marseilles and Barcelona. It seemed that Constantinople's new breed of captive bureaucrats might inherit the Ottoman Empire by default. But that was not to be. The eighteenth century witnessed a last astonishing resurgence of Turkish arms, which recovered the Peloponnesus from Venice and even fought the growing power of Russia to a draw.

Moscow was the "Third Rome," according to Russian Orthodox tradition. Catherine the Great hoped to capture the "Second Rome" (Constantinople) and set her grandson Constantine upon its throne. To this end, she stirred up abortive revolutions within Greece and launched various campaigns southward against the Turks. But all she got for those efforts was a final treaty containing two concessions of importance to the Greeks. The first concession allowed Greek merchantmen to trade under the Russian flag. That helped Greek commerce considerably. The second concession gave foreign governments the privilege of making representations to the Sublime Porte on behalf of its Greek subjects. That amounted to a free charter for an international chess game of intrigue in which the Greeks might serve as willing or unwilling pawns.

Far away in America, men were creating a new and independent na-

tion based in part upon ancient Athenian ideals. Among the Founding Fathers of the United States, James Madison in particular was fond of citing Greek precedents. Moreover, he knew how to take warning from classical mistakes. In *The Federalist* papers, Madison contrasted the organization of the United States Senate with that of the ancient Athenian Assembly. "What bitter anguish," he concluded, "would not the people of Athens have often escaped, if their government had contained so provident a safeguard against the tyranny of their own passions? Popular liberty might then have escaped the indelible reproach of decreeing to the same citizens, the hemlock on one day, and statues the next."

The French Revolution, with its cry for liberty, equality, and fraternity, roused the Greeks as it did oppressed peoples everywhere. Napoleon's campaigns, finally, brought patriotism to a new pitch in Europe. Greeks living in the great European capitals found their own thoughts set alight and transformed into hope. The most optimistic and fiery expatriate of them all was the song writer Constantine Rhigas, who founded the Philiki Hetairia ("Friendly Society") to smuggle arms and money into Greece. Rhigas wrote a Greek version of the *Marseillaise* and formed a collection of stirring Greek ballads as well. These were passed from hand to hand in manuscript. The island cliffs and the high mountainsides of Greece would echo and re-echo with Rhigas' songs during the struggles which lay ahead. He himself, however, did not live to hear them. In 1798 he was captured and shot.

Adamantios Korais was the philosopher of Greece's coming revolution. He lived mostly in France, where he devoted himself to literary pursuits and propaganda. He envisioned a Greek nation of the future which would be defined by language and religion. It was Korais who first called upon his countrymen to remember and revive the glories of classical Greece. Native legend did not hark back so far as that. Most Greek patriots of the early nineteenth century were aware of vanished Byzantium, and that possessed a fairytale glimmer for them. Yet, from their viewpoint, classical Greece had barely existed.

Modern Greek is as close to Homer as modern English is to Chaucer. In other words, Greek has retained considerable continuity over a much longer span than other contemporary tongues. Korais never tired of pointing out the fact. "Education, education and still more educa-

Battle scenes, painted on wood, of the Greek struggle for independence in the 1820s, show blue-coated Hellenes bravely fighting red-uniformed Turks.

tion!" he cried. He saw that to be the only possible salvation of the Greek people.

Korais personally labored to create an artificial Greek tongue half-way between the language of Plato and colloquial *demotiki*. Korais' "reformed" way of writing reduced Slavic and Turkish importations to a minimum. It was to become the basis of future education in Greece. The greatest Greek writers, such as Nikos Kazantzakis, have all preferred the living grit and suppleness of *demotiki* to Korais' bloodless "reformed" variety of Greek. Yet school papers, newspapers, and government pronouncements from Athens all are still written according to the rules he first laid down.

The Congress of Vienna in 1815 was a disappointment for all Greek patriots. "What is Greece?" the Austrian statesman Prince Metternich demanded; no one could give him a precise reply. The Great Powers generally favored peace and quiet, so liberty for Greece was not even discussed. "Pacification" was the word used instead. In order to maintain a proper balance of power, European leaders agreed, the crumbling Ottoman Empire should be somehow shored up.

Six years later, on the twenty-fifth of March, 1821, Archbishop Germanos of Patras raised a new blue and white banner and proclaimed Greek independence. The date is still celebrated as Greece's national holiday. The archbishop's brave gesture was the signal for a terrible massacre of Turkish overlords and their families. By way of immediate reprisal, the sultan hanged the patriarch of Constantinople.

Russian policy was always to press for a gateway to the Mediterranean Sea. Alexander, Tsar of All the Russias, ruled the only great Orthodox Christian power. His foreign minister was a Greek liberal born on the island of Corfu, named John Capodistrias. Those factors, taken together with the tragic certainty that the revolutionaries could never succeed on their own, persuaded everyone that Russia would settle the issue by moving decisively against the sultan. Great historic movements may be turned, however, by purely personal things; especially in an autocracy. Tsar Alexander had come to distrust social unrest; he did practically nothing for the Greek cause. Capodistrias, forced into retirement from the Russian government, settled in Switzerland in order to raise money for the revolutionaries.

The Greeks found an unlooked-for ally in the Epirus region of

northwestern Greece. That area was under the control of a sly, ruthless Albanian named Ali Pasha, who chose to secede from the Ottoman Empire. With some difficulty, the Turks crushed Ali Pasha's rebellion. By then, however, the Peloponnesus and a good many Greek islands were in Greek hands.

The revolutionaries were both blessed and cursed in their leadership. Among the klephts who bore the brunt of the land fighting were Odysseus Androutsos of Boeotia, Marko Bozzaris, and Theodoros Kolokotronis. Such men did battle only when it suited them, being inveterate guerrilla warriors. They also made temporary arrangements with the enemy as a matter of policy. This was not treason to the infant Greek nation, since the very concept of nationhood was itself foreign to the thinking of the klephts. Their basic motivation was simply to free the sacred mountains of mainland Greece from the turbaned tax collector and the shadow of the Turkish crescent. To topple every Moslem minaret in sight, and set glittering crosses upon all the peaks in Greece, was their ambition; never to form a government.

The island leaders, likewise, cherished ambitions far removed from the liberal and nationalistic sentiments of Western intellectuals at the time. Pavlos Koundouriotis of Hydra, and such intrepid sea captains as Konstantinos Kanaris and Andreas Miaoulis formed a saltwater freemasonry. Their small, swift coastal brigs, manned by volunteers from the island villages, made havoc of Turkish sea communications. The islanders' most effective weapon was a wildly courageous trick. They would load a rotten hulk to the gunwales with ammunition, and sail it by night against a Turkish fleet. Before making contact, the Greeks would abandon ship and pull away in their longboats. The fireship exploded, if all went well, in the midst of the enemy. The cheers of Greek sailors on such occasions were not for God and country so much as for freedom of the sea—and no Turkish duties to pay.

Orthodox Greek churchmen who fought on the side of revolution had their own ideas of how the struggle should end; and these again bore little relation to the new winds of patriotism and democracy. Bishop Germanos of Patras, who had first raised the revolutionary flag, journeyed to Rome to seek an audience with the pope. Since the Turks had hanged the Orthodox patriarch at Constantinople, it seemed a good time to attempt once more a reconciliation with the Church of

Rome. The pope, however, flatly refused to see the Greek delegation.

Greek aristocrats who took part in the fighting came closest, oddly enough, to sharing the democratic ideals so often proclaimed in the West. Among them was the island prince Dimitrius Ypsilanti (for whom Ypsilanti, Michigan, was to be named), and the erstwhile Phanariots Theodoros Negris and Alexandros Mavrokordatos. Prince Mavrokordatos had met Lord Byron in Italy, and the two had become fast friends. The eventual triumph of the Greek cause was to grow most especially from that friendship.

Tsar Alexander, Prince Metternich, Lord Castlereagh in England, and the pope, one and all regarded the birth pangs of modern Greece with indifference verging on contempt. Authority had no wish to be disturbed by unseemly cries and groans from Europe's southeastern quarter. European artists, philosophers, and poets, though, heard and responded. This set a new and hopeful precedent for creative men who wish to have some good effect upon history.

Goethe, Schiller, and Victor Hugo stood among the true friends of Greece abroad. So did the painter Eugène Delacroix, one of whose masterpieces depicted a Turkish massacre on the island of Chios. Percy Bysshe Shelley, and especially Lord Byron, spoke in their time as they still speak in eternity for Greek virtues. As Byron wrote:

> *The mountains look on Marathon—*
> *And Marathon looks on the sea;*
> *And musing there an hour alone,*
> *I dreamed that Greece might still be free;*
> *For standing on the Persians' grave,*
> *I could not deem myself a slave.*

Divisions between the various Greek leaders in the struggle were inevitable, and they shattered the impetus of the revolution. The sultan at Constantinople felt powerless to revenge himself fully upon his erstwhile Greek subjects in the Peloponnesus, and so he called upon a semiautonomous Egyptian vassal to do the job. This was Mehemet Ali Pasha, who commanded the strongest remaining land and sea forces in the Moslem world. Mehemet's fleet far outmatched the Greek privateers. He seized Crete, and then set his son Ibrahim ashore on the Peloponnesus with ten thousand men. This expeditionary force

crushed Greek resistance everywhere except for a few mountain fast-nesses and fortified points.

The small port of Missolonghi on the western coast of central Greece held out longest. Surrounded by shallow lagoons, and defended by an heroic populace, it staved off hugely superior forces. Byron, who had landed there as a volunteer, died of a fever at Missolonghi. His old comrade, Mavrokordatos, was in command. In April, 1826, when the bastion finally collapsed, its remaining defenders blew themselves sky-high rather than surrender. Missolonghi is a fishing village today. The mud of its tidal flats still lies thick with shot and shell and human bones. A modest monument commemorates the martyrdom of the old town—an event which at last aroused the conscience of Europe.

The year after Missolonghi's fall, Great Britain, France, and Russia put a combined fleet in Greek waters. Its orders were to practice "peaceful intimidation." The allies' real mission was twofold. First, they meant to force the withdrawal of Ibrahim's forces; and secondly, they hoped to shelter the autonomous creation of a Greek state. The allied fleet commanders sought a conference with Ibrahim, whose own navy they first bottled up in Navarino Bay. When they sent a longboat inshore to begin negotiations, the proud Egyptians opened fire on it. Thereupon, the allied fleet majestically entered the bay with all guns blazing. In the four hours which followed no fewer than sixty ships were sunk—every one of them on the Egyptian side. With this battle, on October 27, 1827, the Greek revolution was over, to all intents won by the belated intervention of Great Britain, France, and Russia.

The Greeks themselves had fought magnificently against enormous odds. They stood victorious, and yet dependent still upon foreign friends. True independence could only come with self-conquest and the resolution of their own internal differences. And such things must always be precarious.

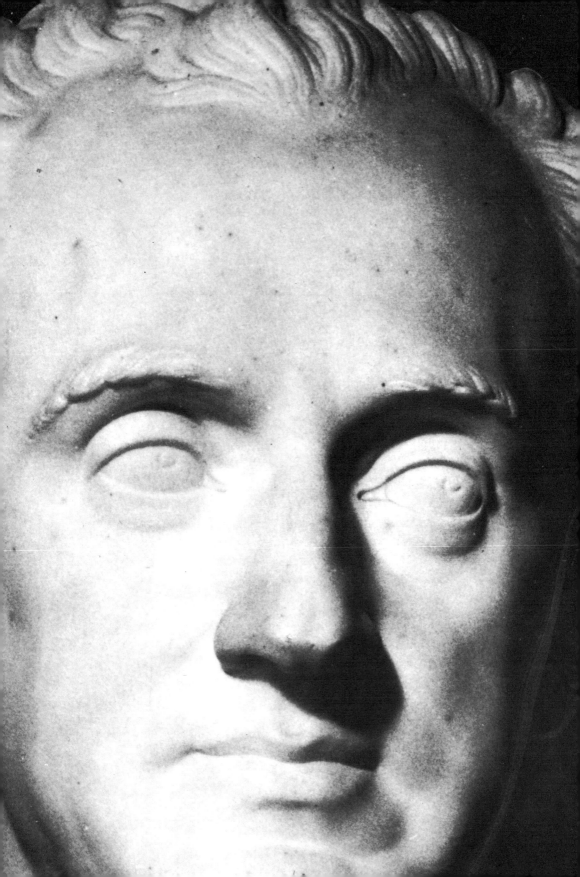

CHAPTER IX

TRIALS AND STRIVINGS OF A SMALL NATION

"The Greeks used to have an Eastern way of life and their purpose was to free themselves from the Turks and to recapture Constantinople. After 1821, they took it upon themselves to overturn things which had been considered sacred and infallible: their Eastern mode of living, women confined to the home, separation of the sexes, much Church-going, much worship of icons, much crossing oneself and repenting one's sins. . . . But afterwards came a greater revolution than the one against the Sultan. Everything was slowly turned upside down, nothing remained in its place, and that is our situation at present."

Thus, rather wistfully, the Greek writer Ion Dragoumis has described his country's rebirth into the modern world. It was traumatic, and the scars still show. In the vastly enlarged mosaic of things today, Greece is rather a tiny and not very important fragment. The young nation's history during the past century and a half has been often tragic, sometimes comic, seldom glorious. Nevertheless, Greece reflects the broad realities of war, politics, and international intrigue as though in a reducing glass.

The first leader of liberated Greece was John Capodistrias, the same

John Capodistrias, ardent nationalist and first president of a liberated Greece

man who had once served as foreign minister to Tsar Alexander. The leaders of the rival Greek parties were reconciled long enough to elect him president in absentia, and he arrived at Nauplia on the Peloponnesus in 1828. Nauplia, the port town of ancient Argos and Mycenae, had been selected as the capital of the new nation. On the day that Capodistrias disembarked there, trouble erupted again, with rival Greek chieftains shooting at each other from opposite quarters of the town. The new president put a stop to that, but it was a bad omen all the same. Bitter factionalism was to be characteristic of the new Greeks. The same restless and bellicose spirit which had brought about interminable wars between the ancient Greek city-states kept threatening to shatter the infant nation. Capodistrias had no choice but to resort to autocratic rule. His whole training and career had been as an authoritarian official in any case, and he was no politician. He thought that if he governed honorably and well, the people might be glad of it. In any event, he antagonized almost everyone.

Great Britain's duke of Wellington held that the new Greek state should be confined to the Peloponnesus alone. Anything larger might become too good a friend of Russia as well as threatening the Balkans and Turkey. Capodistrias argued against that viewpoint. First, he explained, a tiny Greece could not protect itself from its neighbors or ever develop a viable economy. Secondly, he insisted, he could not possibly restrain his irregular Greek troops from attempting to liberate their brothers of the mainland and the islands. In fact he had no wish to restrain them. Capodistrias sent his best captains in all directions with confidential orders to seize what territories they could. Mavrokordatos tried and failed to secure the island of Crete. A philhellene French commander named Charles Nicolas Fabvier did no better at Chios. Dimitrius Ypsilanti, however, marched northward through Attica and Boeotia to win the final battle of the war near Thebes in the autumn of 1829. By the London Protocol of 1830, Greece was recognized as sovereign and independent. The new state was declared by the European powers to consist of the Peloponnesus, central Greece, and the Cyclades islands, but it excluded Thessaly, Crete, Samos, and other areas incontrovertibly Greek although still under Turkish rule.

Russia, France, and England stationed resident commissioners at Nauplia with powers to interfere in Capodistrias' government. The

klepht chieftains kept all their pride and much of their wartime power. The same held true for the merchant princes and freebooters of the Aegean Islands. The erstwhile Phanariots and Europe-trained aristocrats pushed hard for a free press and for the convocation of a democratic assembly. The clergy complained of its ideological subjection to the new Orthodox patriarch at Constantinople, since he reigned from the sultan's lap as it were. The peasantry had no spokesman, but it appears that they were taxed to the limit of endurance. (Thousands of peasants made the silently eloquent protest of emigrating to Turkish territories.) Caught between so many conflicting interests, Capodistrias picked his way as best he could. For three and a half years the beleaguered president held on. Then, one Sunday morning as he walked to church in Nauplia, an assassin's bullet cut Capodistrias down.

Russia, France, and England thereupon selected a seventeen-year-old Bavarian prince named Otto to rule Greece. Otto arrived at Nauplia aboard a British frigate in the year 1833. He brought with him three Bavarian "regents" to be the government, plus 3,500 Bavarian troops to maintain order.

Otto's regents speedily dissolved the irregular bands of armed Greeks which had been disrupting the new nation. They also cut the Greek clergy free from dependence on the patriarch at Constantinople, and made it a tool of the Greek state instead. Finally, they managed to evict a die-hard Turkish garrison from the Acropolis at Athens, which then became Otto's capital. Athens built a grand Germanic palace for the king, and near it a university. The old klepht revolutionary leader Kolokotronis looked from the university to the palace and remarked: "This house will eat that house!" Kolokotronis meant of course that new generations of university-educated politicians were sure to threaten the monarchy; and he was right.

Otto meanwhile managed to achieve a small measure of popularity. Three things, however, counted against him. First, he refused to renounce his Roman Catholic faith in favor of Orthodoxy. Second, his queen, Amalie of Oldenburg, remained both childless and Protestant. Third, he refused to call the promised National Assembly, which was to draft a constitution, until forced by a bloodless revolution in 1843.

That uprising established constitutional monarchy. But, sadly enough, Otto's Greek army officers and parliamentarians proved to be

very nearly as highhanded as the Bavarians before them. They led Greece into various embarrassing confrontations with foreign powers, culminating in a British blockade of Athens' port, the Piraeus, in 1850. Such foreign pressures always defeated Otto. Yet he earned a reputation as the champion of something to which Greeks could respond. Echoing the thoughts which Adamantios Korais had propagated in the previous century, he proclaimed that his kingdom ought by rights to include all those people who spoke Greek and professed the Orthodox religion. This *Megali Idea,* or "Great Idea," was to have a dangerously heady influence.

Otto himself could only pay it lip service. His halfhearted attempt to gain something for Greece by taking Russia's part against Turkey was frustrated from the start. The British controlled the Mediterranean and they openly despised Otto. The Greeks, too, turned against him finally. In 1862 Otto and Queen Amalie returned from a cruise on the royal yacht to find Athens once again in revolt. Protesting their love for Greece, they sailed away to Germany. Otto had reigned for thirty years and accomplished nothing of note.

The Greek National Assembly passed a resolution requesting Queen Victoria's second son, Prince Alfred, to come and be king. The request was refused. Denmark, however, provided a substitute. Prince William George, an amiable Dane of eighteen, mounted the Greek throne in 1863. He was crowned "George the First, King of the Hellenes." His title was significant. It meant that the Greeks were now committed to their Great Idea, for good or ill. George claimed kingship of a whole people. The fact that more than half his ostensible subjects lived beyond the territorial borders of Greece would simply have to be worked out as time went by. The British gave his reign an auspicious start by freely ceding Corfu and other Ionian islands in their possession to the Greek crown.

George himself began with a bold stroke. One of his first acts as king was to insist that the National Assembly finish drafting a more democratic constitution than the one in force. This not only provided for a single house of parliament to be elected by secret ballot of all adult male Greek subjects, but also curtailed patronage. The great estates held by the Church and the old revolutionary families were to be largely broken up. Except for the royal house no aristocratic titles or

The Orthodox parish priest still plays a vital role in modern Greece.

pretensions were to be allowed validity. The effort was to create a class-less society of small landholders and merchants, all of them voters but ruled from a throne. That arrangement worked well in Scandinavia. Would it also prove satisfactory for so clannish, impoverished, and explosive a people as the Greeks?

Rival leaders, the budget-minded conservative Kharilaos Trikoupis, and the flag-waving expansionist Theodoros Delijannis, sought to command Greek destiny. King George leaned in Delijannis' direction. Trikoupis, however, impressed upon the king the argument that royal preference ought not to decide the selection of a prime minister. That was up to parliament, after all. George took the point with reasonable grace. Thereafter Trikoupis and Delijannis alternated in power.

Delijannis' policy was to fish the troubled waters of the Balkan states to gain northern territories for Greece. Russia's pan-Slavic paternalism and the sultan's divide-and-conquer policy largely checkmated his campaigns, although Thessaly was added to the kingdom. Other northern regions in dispute were an ethnographer's nightmare. Greeks, Turks, Vlachs, Serbs, Slavs, and Bulgars mingled in Macedonia, for example. The mixture there gave rise to the French word for a fruit salad: *macédoine.*

After every setback to the Great Idea, Trikoupis would be voted into office once again and would immediately clamp down hard on finances. The Piraeus was now fourth in importance among Mediterranean ports, but Greece remained poverty-stricken. Interest on loans from abroad accounted for no less than a third of the national budget, and chronic unemployment plagued the nation. Hundreds of thousands of Greeks emigrated to more promising lands, especially the United States, over the years.

Toward the close of the nineteenth century, the islanders of Crete at last succeeded in expelling their Ottoman oppressors. The Cretans then proclaimed their firm desire for *enosis* ("union") with Greece. The Great Powers refused to allow that. Reluctantly, therefore, the government of Athens disowned Cretan ambitions. A near revolt of the Greek army was the result. By 1909 the question of what to do about Crete threatened to plunge all Greece into a civil war. At the eleventh hour, the leader of the Cretan insurgents was invited to Athens for consultations. Eleutherios ("Freedom") Venizelos would prove to be by far

the most brilliant and persuasive personage in modern Greek history. His capacity for seizing victory from the jaws of defeat was reminiscent of a great ancient Athenian: Themistocles.

Politics in Greece had come to involve a triangular struggle. There were three separate centers of power, each one possessing strengths and weaknesses. The first was the royal house. Its symbolic glamor, international connections, and partial command of public loyalty were vitiated, in the nature of things, by personal conceit and arbitrariness. The second was parliament. Its strength lay in its awareness of the public will; its weaknesses were inefficiency, division of purpose, and a habit of personal patronage which no legislation could kill. A typical parliamentarian would have dozens of relatives, hundreds of cronies, and possibly thousands of "godchildren" to care for. Personal promises, both given and received, commanded his vote as a rule. The third force in Greek politics was the army. Its strength lay not only in guns but also in the fact that it remained the most highly organized body. Its weaknesses, of course, were the old Spartan faults of harsh, unimaginative ruthlessness.

Venizelos persuaded the leaders of all three power centers that he could do something for each one as prime minister. Duly elected to that office in the year 1910, he set Greece on a course of hope dominated by the Great Idea. His first move was to invite a French army mission and a British navy mission to Greece for the purpose of modernizing the Greek armed forces. His second move was in the realm of international diplomacy. Venizelos pasted together an unlikely alliance with the Balkan states on his northern border. The object of this exercise was to challenge what remained of Ottoman power on the European scene. In 1912 Greece, Serbia, Montenegro, and Bulgaria marched together against the Turks. They won, for Turkey was in disarray. Venizelos saw to it that among the spoils of the "Balkan Wars" the southern Epirus, Macedonia, and part of Thrace fell to Greece. Not only that, but he finally persuaded the Great Powers to recognize Crete and the island of Samos as Greek territory. Thus he nearly doubled Greek dominions within a very few years and at a small cost in blood and treasure. Venizelos accomplished all this without drawing more than a frown or two from the Great Powers, without causing undue chagrin to his Balkan allies, and even without real harshness to the Turks.

OVERLEAF: *Villagers from Lia, in northwestern Greece, pause to gossip at a local* cafénion, *a combination outdoor café and grocery store.*

Constantinople was the Turkish prize for which all Greece traditionally longed, yet Venizelos had the restraint not to grab for it. He thought Constantinople ought perhaps to be an "Open City," sacred to Christian and Moslem equally. Since that could not be brought about (although he was to press for it after the First World War) he left the city peacefully under Ottoman control. Venizelos knew that a statesman may achieve greatness not only by dint of positive accomplishments but also by restraint.

In 1913, the fiftieth year of his reign, King George died by a mad assassin's bullet. Crown Prince Constantine, who had earned distinction as commander in chief of the Greek army during the Balkan Wars, ascended the throne. A conflict of world-wide dimensions loomed ahead. The new monarch, sadly for his country, had married a sister of Germany's Kaiser Wilhelm. Himself a military man, Constantine viewed the Kaiser's crack land armies with considerable awe. Greece had better keep in Germany's good graces, he decided. Venizelos disagreed, for two reasons. First, during the struggle to come, Great Britain, France, and Italy were certain to dominate the Mediterranean. That put Greece in the power of the democratic Allies. Second, and more important by far, not Germany but the Allies would have right on their side.

King Constantine declined to accept those arguments. He dissolved parliament and dismissed Venizelos from office. That split the country. With Allied help Venizelos instituted a rival government at Thessalonike. Most of the newly won territories sided with him. Yet times were very dark; Germany seemed to be winning. The free democracies tried and failed to force the Dardanelles at Gallipoli. Then, to secure their Greek flank, they squeezed Constantine out. The king managed to avoid making a formal abdication, but he retired to Switzerland. Venizelos thereupon reconvened the previous parliament at Athens.

In a truly historic nine-hour address, Venizelos outlined the position and international responsibilities of Greece. Receiving parliament's vote of confidence, he proceeded to mobilize and deploy a quarter of a million Greek troops. These played an honorable part in the final defeat of the Kaiser's forces.

At the Versailles Peace Conference which followed, Venizelos charmed all parties and obtained dangerous new concessions for

Greece. The most important of these was a Greek enclave including the port city of Smyrna on Turkey's Aegean coast. Venizelos hoped Smyrna would prove to be a refuge for the Greeks under Turkish domination in Anatolia, but things did not work out that way.

While Venizelos was abroad, his opponents in parliament ordered a plebiscite which called for King Constantine's return. The plebiscite may well have been rigged, but Constantine thought it gave him a mandate to launch a full-scale attack upon Turkey. The newly acquired port of Smyrna provided him with a convenient base. Constantine's troops were stunningly beaten, however, and thrown back upon Smyrna. Some fifty thousand Greek soldiers lost their lives in the campaign. Many times that number of Greek-speaking inhabitants of Anatolia were slaughtered in the civilian massacres which followed. These disasters took place in 1921, on the hundredth anniversary of the Greek Declaration of Independence. Still worse was to come. The enraged Turks sacked Smyrna and burned it to the ground. King Constantine abdicated in disgrace, and died soon afterward. An army junta seized power from the nonplussed Athenian parliament. Its first act was to execute a general and five former cabinet ministers as scapegoats. Having shocked public opinion everywhere, the junta appointed Venizelos to pick up the pieces in a conference with the Turks at Lausanne, Switzerland.

In that cool climate, far away from their embittered and still bloodthirsty compatriots, the conferees concluded one of the most remarkable international agreements on record. Venizelos negotiated a lopsided exchange of populations. A million and a quarter Greeks in Anatolia were to trade homelands with four hundred thousand Turks in Greek territories.

The forcible relocation of so many families was agonizing, naturally, and the vast flood of refugees pouring into Greece put an almost intolerable strain upon the Greek economy. Yet even so, the exchange worked well. The chief excuse for conflict between Greece and Turkey was forever removed.

On the strength of this master stroke, Venizelos returned temporarily to power. He was to serve a good many more times as prime minister, but Venizelos' great days were over. Never again did he succeed in making parliament, the royal house, and the army pull together.

Parliament became his personal power base. When army leaders took over the country, and when Constantine's son mounted the throne as George II, Venizelos suffered exile. Shortly before his death in 1936, the old man sent from Paris a stream of letters urging opponents to cooperate with each other.

At that point Greece had passed under the firm control of an army general named Ioannis Metaxas, who feared Venizelos alone among men. Metaxas sternly vetoed plans for the great persuader's body to be shipped home to Athens. Venizelos' motionless and silent remains might cause a riot, he explained. Metaxas' dictatorship was modeled unabashedly upon that of Mussolini. He went so far as to censor one of Sophocles' tragedies and Thucydides' account of the Peloponnesian

In the time-tested way of her ancestors, an old woman places a cake in the community fourno, *a beehive-shaped oven of baked mud.*

War as being "too democratic." In the practical realm, he built roads and steadily strengthened the Greek army. His fascism was strictly for home consumption, and Metaxas carefully avoided aligning Greece with the Axis powers.

On an October night in 1940, Metaxas attended a party at the Italian Legation in Athens. He seemed cordial enough, despite the tension brought about by Italy's recent occupation of Albania. Early next morning, the Italian minister paid a surprise visit to Metaxas' residence. The general, clad in a bathrobe, opened the front door himself. "We need your immediate permission," the minister said, "for our troops to cross the Albanian border into Greece." Metaxas, standing in the open doorway, thought that over quietly for a second or two. It meant joining the Axis and acknowledging subservience to Mussolini. The Italian army was highly regarded at the time. Tilting back his head just a little and raising his eyebrows slightly, Metaxas said: *"Ochi!"* The word means No. Gently, the general shut the door in the face of Mussolini's minister. The date when this occurred, October 28, is still a national festival. The Greek people celebrate it as "Ochi Day."

Hostilities began that very afternoon. To the amazement of the world, Metaxas' troops forced the Italians step by step far back across the mountains of Albania. Mussolini's military prestige received a blow from which it was never to recover. General Metaxas died in bed the following winter. Then, with the coming of spring, German dive bombers, paratroops, and tanks descended upon Greece. Hitler had decided to occupy the country in order to prepare a southern screen for his attack upon Russia.

This time, Greek defenses were speedily overwhelmed. However, the occupying German, Italian, and Bulgarian troops found Greece a thorny land. As in the days of Turkish domination, the mountain fastnesses remained largely free. Guerillas swooped at night to destroy isolated garrisons. Underground resistance made even city streets unsafe for troopers after dark. Retaliation for all this was savage. Mass executions of civilian hostages occurred. Such measures only strengthened Greek hatred.

Then, little by little, a split appeared between the ranks of the resistance fighters. One group, led by ex-officers of the regular army, remained loyal to King George II and his government in exile in Cairo.

The other group fought more ferociously, on the whole, and found better support among the peasantry and the urban proletariat. The leaders of this second group were liberals and radicals who opposed the monarchy on principle. What little loyalty to outside forces they possessed was mainly reserved for the ogre in the Kremlin: Joseph Stalin.

As Axis fortunes everywhere began to wane, the Greeks turned upon each other. The left-wing resistance forces gained the upper hand. British troops poured in to hold Athens, at least, for the return of the legitimate government in exile. It seemed, however, that the whole country would soon go Communist.

What turned the tide was the Truman Doctrine, announced in March of 1947. President Truman pledged massive United States assistance in money and arms to help Greece and Turkey resist the Communist menace. He dispatched General James Van Fleet to organize counter attacks upon the insurgents. Perceiving that the Americans were serious, Stalin decided to abide by the Yalta Agreement which placed Greece and Turkey outside his sphere of influence. Marshal Tito of Yugoslavia meanwhile closed his Greek border to the rebels. They found themselves crushed, as it were, against the Iron Curtain. By spring of 1949, the civil war was over. It had taken an even higher toll than the Axis occupation of Greece.

George II was dead by then. His younger brother Paul reigned as monarch of the Hellenes. Paul well understood where his true power lay. "You belong to me," he said to his army officers, "and I belong to you." The Crown and the military together dominated parliament. General Alexander Papagos served in highly authoritarian style as prime minister. He made Greece a southeastern anchor of the North Atlantic Treaty Organization.

Rhodes and the smaller Dodecanese islands, which had been Italian for most of the century, were now Greek at last. The large island of Cyprus, southeast of Rhodes, remained British. Great Britain wished to hold on to Cyprus as a naval and air station in the eastern Mediterranean. One out of five Cypriots, the island's Turkish minority, had no great objection to British rule. The remaining islanders were Greek in language and religion; they longed for union with Greece. Strikes, riots, terrorism, and civil war were among the methods employed toward that goal. Not until 1960 was a compromise solution agreed

upon. Cyprus became a republic, independent of both Great Britain and Greece. The island's Orthodox patriarch, Makarios, took the office of president. Makarios was to dominate Cyprus for a long time to come. However, "the Cyprus question" was far from being settled to everyone's satisfaction.

The death of General Papagos in 1955 had signaled no change for Greece. King Paul had appointed one of the general's protégés, black-browed Constantine Karamanlis, to be the new prime minister. Karamanlis was to keep the nation steadily on course for an unprecedented eight years of calm, although the calm was somewhat artificially produced. It depended on continuing aid from abroad combined with rather repressive measures at home.

Cracks in the structure headed by Karamanlis began to appear in 1962, when the United States cut off economic assistance to Greece. Bitter strikes occurred. King Paul, his German queen Frederika, and their children were openly attacked as a drain on the nation's slender treasury. In 1963 a pacifist named Grigorios Lambrakis was murdered on the street following a left-wing rally. The Thessalonike police appeared to have connived at the murder. A liberal parliamentarian named George Papandreou publicly accused Karamanlis of being "morally responsible" for Lambrakis' death. Karamanlis answered the charge with an inapposite and yet wonderfully dignified remark. Papandreou would be "ashamed all his life," he said, having made such a suggestion. The peculiar strength of Greek character is to be personal at all times. Conversely, this has always been the bane of Greek politics.

Later that same year, Karamanlis seized the occasion of a trivial quarrel with King Paul to resign his post and retire to Paris. Free elections followed, and resulted in a stunning victory for George Papandreou.

King Paul, suffering from cancer of the stomach, lived only long enough to swear in the new government. The crown prince ascended the throne as Constantine II. He was twenty-three years old, a yachtsman and karate expert, married to a pretty Danish princess. Papandreou, old enough to be the king's grandfather, treated Constantine with easy indulgence.

The new prime minister began with everything on his side. He possessed a popular mandate to loosen the reins of government and cut

back the military budget. His son Andreas, who had been teaching at the University of California, came home to help his father introduce a series of long-overdue reforms. Scientific methods of analysis and management were needed to replace old-fashioned patronage. The test of nations now appeared to be social justice and economic viability.

For the moment, the Papandreous and parliament had won their power struggle with the Crown and the army. The prime minister pushed his luck, however, when he accused the army of having fraudulently engineered Karamanlis' victory in a previous election. The military struck back very obliquely by "discovering" a conspiracy in its own ranks. The name given to the conspiracy was *Aspida* ("Shield"). It was said to involve hundreds of lower-ranking officers bent on destruction of the monarchy. The leader of the plot, supposedly, was none other than Andreas Papandreou. Did this charge contain any truth at all? The answer may never be known for certain.

George Papandreou's own response to this at least partially manufactured crisis was to make an urgent grab for the Defense Portfolio. If his son were to be tried for treason, he wanted to be personally in charge of the investigation. King Constantine stepped in. The young monarch called upon Papandreou to appoint a disinterested minister of defense who would proceed with a full-scale inquiry into *Aspida*. Papandreou thereupon resigned, but only as a political maneuver. He had every expectation of being swept back into power very soon. The majority of the people were with him still. Widespread rallies, strikes, and riots demonstrated that. The king and the army sponsored various caretaker governments, only to see each one topple. At last a general election was set for May of 1967. This, Papandreou would have won hands down, according to most observers. But it was not to happen.

In the early hours of the morning of April 21st, the phone rang in King Constantine's country palace at Tatoi. The king got out of bed to learn that tanks were rumbling through the streets of Athens. He telephoned a trusted minister, who told him: "Soldiers are breaking in my door right now." Then the phone went dead. Tanks ringed the parliament building and every other key point in Athens. More than six thousand people, including most political figures of importance, were arrested before dawn. George and Andreas Papandreou were among those taken into custody. King Constantine meanwhile telephoned to

The elderly devout, wearing somber mourning attire, attend a church service in a northern Greek village.

his air force command and ordered that a helicopter be sent to Tatoi. It never came. Army detachments moved into position around the palace grounds. They were there to protect the king, it was explained. Constantine and his pregnant queen went for a predawn walk in the garden. They could not guess what had occurred. There seemed nothing to do but wait.

Among its many contingency plans, NATO had produced one code-named "Prometheus" to deal with any serious threat of a Communist takeover in Greece. The generals felt that they might be compelled to use this against Papandreou. The plan had been carefully dusted off and updated for the purpose. This gave a golden opportunity to a handful of conspirators in the second echelon of the army. Colonel George Papadopoulos, a psychological warfare specialist, deliberately jumped the gun when he set "Prometheus" in operation. His coconspirators were an intelligence colonel named Nicholas Markarezos, and Brigadier Stylianos Patakos. The brigadier, trained partly at Fort Dix in the United States, commanded the tank forces in the Athens area. When his tanks began rolling through Athens to implement "Prometheus," the top generals of the army were asleep in their beds at home.

Next day, the few generals who balked at taking orders from their former inferiors, found themselves on the retired list. The coup had been accomplished almost without bloodshed. It was a chillingly smooth operation and a credit to the impersonal efficiency of the nameless NATO officials responsible for its planning. King Constantine raged at the conspirators, but on second thought he lent his name to the initial stages of their regime. This was of crucial importance to Greece's international relations. Since all foreign ambassadors were accredited to the king, they automatically "recognized" the new regime.

The situation was, however, claustrophobic for the Crown. "The colonels" had entirely destroyed Constantine's influence together with the power of their own erstwhile commanders who had been loyal to him. Constantine found this out when he flew to the north of Greece to attempt a countercoup. His gesture was futile; it got no support from anyone. Thereupon he fled to Rome with his family. Although relieved to see him go, the commanders still paid lip service to the monarchy.

George Papadopoulos soon emerged as the strong man of the revolutionary regime. Patakos, an amiable and even humorous puritan,

served as its chief spokesman. Some government decrees, such as the ones which outlawed long hair for males and ordered regular attendance at church, made the world laugh a little. They were soon rescinded, but strict censorship and bans on strikes and on public meetings remained in force.

"The colonels" made no pretense of loving democracy. As Brigadier Patakos gently explained: "Parliamentarians lie for votes." International insistence that the government of Greece hold free elections naturally fell upon deaf ears. Cries for release of political prisoners met with greater success as time went by.

The sad fact is that every government of modern Greece has been guilty of holding political prisoners in considerable numbers. "The colonels" refrained from executing anyone, but they did cram Greek jails and penal islands to the bursting point at first. They cracked down totally upon the extreme left wing, harshly upon middle-of-the-road politicians, and selectively upon right-wing elitists. Their main motive, however, seemed to be intimidation as against permanent repression.

Beatings took place. Then came release for all but a so-called "hard core of Communists." George Papandreou had been jailed before, by the Nazis. This time he suffered house arrest. His son Andreas chose exile to Paris. So did the best Greek composer of modern times, Mikis Theodorakis, an outspoken Communist. Theodorakis' music, incidentally, was banned from Greece. Artists and intellectuals such as the actress Melina Mercouri, the novelist Vassilis Vassilikos, and the publisher Helen Vlachos were stripped of Greek citizenship. They also continued agitating from abroad for the "liberation" of Greece. But Greeks had suffered too much from each other. No one really wished for yet another civil war.

Paradoxically, perhaps, the stiff new broom swung with such energy by Papadopoulos brought an economic upsurge to Greece. Foreign investments and tourist revenues dramatically improved. The tide of economic chaos, which had lapped dangerously close, slowly receded. This meant a lot to Greeks at home, who had in fact been better acquainted with hunger than with freedom. Greeks tended to discuss their new dictator in the same wryly apathetic tones that Englishmen reserve for the weather. Like chilly scenes of winter, the Papadopoulos regime appeared quite unavoidable.

EPILOGUE

The Greeks have a word, *philotimo,* which is generally translated as "self-esteem." It is, however, untranslatable. The overtones of the word are inviolability and freedom in an inward sense. *Philotimo* reflects the dignity of being an individual person, that is to say unique. If the Greek people have anything in common besides language and religion, individualism is it. Their pagan ancestors feared the gods without bowing down to them. Modern Greeks, too, fear many things; and with good reason. Yet, as individuals, they bow down to none. To call this basic attitude "democratic" would not be right. Easy familiarity is not part of it, nor is submission to the popular will. The Greek tends to recognize authority of any kind as something external. It cannot be allowed to impinge upon his psyche. When that does happen, he becomes dangerously angry in a deeply personal way. The New York drug addict who attempts to hold up a Greek candy store and gets himself shot by the proprietor has unwittingly aroused the man's *philotimo.* Similarly, when King Agamemnon seized a slave girl from Achilles on the Trojan plain, he precipitated a crisis of *philotimo* in the hero's soul. The first few pages of Homer's *Iliad,* therefore, go straight to the core of all things Greek.

Glancing back, now, over the history of Greece, one can distinguish three basic aspects. It exhibits chronic turbulence, amazing continuity, and truly miraculous creativity. On the surface those three would seem contradictory. What unites them is *philotimo.*

The turbulence of Greece begins at least as far back as the eruption of Thera three and a half thousand years ago. The Mycenaean and Dorian civilizations which followed that Bronze Age disaster elevated warfare to a matter of honor. The test of excellence came to be killing one's man. This idea helped the Greeks defy Persian invaders in the fifth century B.C., but it condemned them to suicidal conflicts at home. In the following century, Alexander the Great carried Greek arms and

culture all the way to India. Then came Roman, Byzantine, Frankish, and Turkish domination. For two thousand years and more, Greece boiled, as it were, under the lid. Regaining independence at last, the Greeks reverted to the internecine struggles and abrupt changes of government which their ancestors had practiced.

The continuity of Greek culture makes a smooth contrast to the zig-zag fortunes of the race. No one can live for long in the Greek country-side without a growing realization that the pagan gods live on. Their names are changed to those of saints and spirits, but every peasant feels their influence. Greek Orthodox Christianity, again, is a pervasive force in realms which no statistics can surround. To take part in an Easter celebration on a Greek island and hear the words *Christos Anesti!* ("Christ is Risen!") ring out at midnight is to learn something which cannot be taught. Finally, the Greek language is extraordinary in its longevity. "All things pass by us, or we pass by them," an ancient Greek poet has written. That statement holds good even for ways of speaking, and yet the fact remains that any Athenian today can read and understand it in the original.

Creativeness is the crowning glory of the Greek race. Struggle on the political plane and even cultural survival as an entity have less signifi-cance than this. The difference being, of course, that the great things which individual Greeks have created benefit all humanity. Homer, Hesiod, Sappho, and Archilochus were only the beginning of a litera-ture which towers above all others in the world. Greek sculptors, paint-ers, and architects accomplished as much again. The Minoan "Harvest Cup" at Heraklion's Archaeological Museum, the "Zeus" at Athens, the Parthenon, Byzantium's Sancta Sophia, and the Chora frescoes in once-Greek Istanbul, highlight a three-thousand-year love-feast of art. Each course in that feast proved to be something new under the sun. The Greek contributions to law, social structure, and science, too, were profoundly original. Greek philosophy from Pythagoras through Plato and Aristotle to Poltinus remains the wonder of the world of intellect. Whoever confronts the basic questions of human existence will find heroic allies among the ancient Greek philosophers.

Is there any one way to account for the continual bubblings and per-vasive blessings of Greek culture? Probably not. They have welled from the secret psyches of individual Greeks, shielded by *philotimo.*

CHRONOLOGY

c. 1700–c. 1400 B.C.	Minoan civilization flourishes in Crete
c. 1400	Mycenae becomes center of powerful civilization
c. 1200	Trojan War; fall of Mycenaean city-states
c. 1150	Beginning of Dorian migrations
c. 1100–c. 1000	Ionian migration to Asia Minor
c. 800–c. 700	Homer, author of the *Iliad, Odyssey*
776	Traditional date of first Olympian Games
c. 750–c. 550	Colonization by Greek city-states
c. 700–c. 600	Hesiod, poet, author of *Theogony, Works and Days*
c. 636–c.546	Thales of Miletus, first known Western philosopher
621	Draco issues severe legal code for Athens
fl. c. 600	Sappho, lyric poetess; Aesop, originator of fable
c. 594	Solon lays foundations of Athenian democracy
c. 582–c. 507	Pythagoras, mathematician and philosopher
546	Cyrus, emperor of Persia, subdues Greek Asia Minor
525–456	Aeschylus, playwright
c. 496–407	Sophocles, playwright
499–479	Persian Wars
c. 485–406	Euripides, playwright
c. 484–425	Herodotus, father of history
469–399	Socrates, philosopher and teacher
c. 460–429	Pericles leads Athens during Golden Age
c. 460–c. 400	Thucydides, historian of Peloponnesian War
454	Treasury of Delian league is moved from Delos to Athens
c. 450–c. 385	Aristophanes, playwright
431–404	Peloponnesian War; Athens surrenders to Sparta
c. 430–c. 354	Xenophon of Athens, historian
c. 428–c. 348	Plato, philosopher and disciple of Socrates
404–371	Sparta fights sporadically with Greek cities and Persia
384–322	Aristotle, philosopher and founder of Lyceum in Athens
384–322	Demosthenes, Athenian orator and statesman
371	Thebes defeats Sparta at Leuctra
359	Philip II assumes Macedonian throne; expands realm
338	Philip defeats Athens and Thebes in battle at Chaeronea; becomes master of Greece
336–323	Alexander the Great reigns; creates empire from Egypt to India
after 323	Alexandria becomes center of Hellenistic world; empire of Alexander the Great is torn apart by his warring generals; frequent warfare among rival Greek leagues

CREDITS AND INDEX

2 Base map drawn by Richard Edes Harrison, courtesy of Ginn and Company, A Xerox Company, Lexington, Mass. 4 Helmet—Courtesy of the Curator, Newstead Abbey; mask—National Archaeological Museum, Athens—D. A. Harissiadis; acrobat—Archaeological Museum, Heraklion; Hassia; Pan—Metropolitan Museum of Art, Rogers Fund 6 National Archaeological Museum, Athens 11 Paul Boissonnas 12 **left** Dumbarton Oaks Collection 12 **right** Museum of Fine Arts, Boston 17 **left** Archaeological Museum, Heraklion 17 **right** Louvre; Giraudon 18 Archaeological Museum, Heraklion; Hassia 21 Archaeological Museum, Heraklion; Hirmer 24 Munich Glypothek—Leonard von Matt 29 National Archaeological Museum, Athens—J. Powell 33 Robert E. Ginna 36–37 Instituto Arti Grafiche, Bergamo 38 Museum, Mykonos; German Archaeological Institute, Athens 41 Louvre—Guiley-Lagache 44–45 Louvre 48 Louvre 50 D. A. Harissiadis 55 Rapho-Guillumette—Hans Hannau 58 Louvre 63 Olympia Museum—Alison Frantz 66–67 Metropolitan Museum of Art, Rogers Fund, 1914 70 Wadsworth Atheneum, Hartford 74 Vatican Museum; Anderson 79 Delphi Museum; Alinari-Viollet 82 **top** D. A. Harissiadis

82 **bot.** Alison Frantz 83 **top** D. A. Harissiadis 83 **bot. left** Carole Muller 83 **bot. right** Alison Frantz 87 Art Museum, Princeton 91 Bibliothèque Nationale, Service Photographique 95 **top** Museo Nazionale di Villa Guilia, Rome 95 **bot.** Louvre; Giraudon 99 Roger-Viollet 101 American School of Classical Studies, Athens 104 Metropolitan Museum of Art, Gift of J. Pierpont Morgan, 1917 107 Metropolitan Museum of Art, Rogers Fund, 1906 111 **clockwise from top** Museum of Fine Arts, Boston; Museum of Fine Arts, Boston; Courtesy of the Trustees of the British Museum; Museum of Fine Arts, Boston; Courtesy of the Trustees of the British Museum 114 National Archaeological Museum, Athens 119 Courtesy of the Trustees of the British Museum 122–23 Foto Teresi 127 George Holton 132 Museo Nazionale, Naples 135 Walter C. Baker Collection, New York 137 Robert von Spallart, *Tableau Historique des Costumes,* 1804 140 Freer Gallery of Art, Smithsonian Institution 144 Museo Nazionale, Naples; Anderson 149 Louvre 152 Landesmuseum, Karlsruhe 153 Kunsthistorischesmuseum, Vienna 156 Bayerisches Staatsmuseum, Munich 159 Alinari 161 Museo Sacro, Biblioteca Vaticana 164 Hirmer

168–69 Biblioteca National, Madrid; Photo Oronoz 173 Bibliothèque Nationale 176 Scala 182 Emmanuel Bernarthos 187 Topkapi Palace Museum—Ara Guler 191 **both** Historical and Ethnological Museum, Athens—D. A. Harissiadis 196 Emmanuel Bernathos 201–213 all Margot Granitsas

Grateful acknowledgment is made for permission to use material from the following works: Aristophanes, A Study, by Gilbert Murray. Published 1933 by the Clarendon Press, Oxford. *Description of Greece,* Vol. III, by Pausanias, translated by W.H.S. Jones. Published 1933 by the Harvard University Press, Cambridge. *The Greek Genius and Its Meaning to Us,* 2nd edition, by R. W. Livingstone. Published 1915 by the Clarendon Press, Oxford. *History of the Peloponnesian War,* by Thucydides, translated by Rex Warner. Published 1954 by Penguin Books Ltd., London. *The Oxford Book of Greek Verse in Translation,* edited by T. F. Higham and C. M. Bowra. Published 1938 by the Clarendon Press, Oxford. *The Rise and Fall of Athens,* by Plutarch, translated by Ian Scott-Kilvert. Copyright © 1960 by Ian Scott-Kilvert. Published 1960 by Penguin Books Ltd., London.

Page numbers in **boldface type** refer to illustrations.
Page references to map entries are in *italic type.*